D1055828

brilliant

retirement

Your practical guide to a happy, healthy,
financially sound retirement

Nic Peeling

Prentice Hall
is an imprint of

Harlow, England • London • New York • Boston • San Francisco • Toronto • Sydney • Singapore • Hong Kong
Tokyo • Seoul • Taipei • New Delhi • Cape Town • Madrid • Mexico City • Amsterdam • Munich • Paris • Milan

PEARSON EDUCATION LIMITED

Edinburgh Gate
Harlow CM20 2JE
Tel: +44 (0)1279 623623
Fax: +44 (0)1279 431059
Website: www.pearsoned.co.uk

First published in Great Britain in 2010

ISBN: 978-0-273-72327-1

British Library Cataloguing-in-Publication Data
A catalogue record for this book is available from the British Library

Library of Congress Cataloging-in-Publication Data
Peeling, Nic.
  Brilliant retirement : everything you need to know and do to make the most
of your golden years / Nic Peeling.
      p. cm.
  ISBN 978-0-273-72327-1 (pbk.)
1.   Retirement.   2.   Retirement--Planning.   I.   Title.
  HQ1062.P435 2010
  646.7'9--dc22

                                                          2010011723

10 9 8 7 6 5 4 3 2 1
14 13 12 11 10

Typeset in 10pt Plantin by 30
Printed and bound in Great Britain by Ashford Colour Press Ltd, Gosport,
Hants

retirement

Contents

Dedication

To my brother Alan

About the author

Nic Peeling has a doctorate from the Computing Laboratory at Oxford University. He joined the Royal Signals and Radar Establishment (RSRE) in 1979 as a research scientist. As RSRE evolved into the Defence Research Agency, and finally a public listed company called QinetiQ, Nic moved from research, through technology exploitation to become a manager and an IT consultant.

In 2007, as QinetiQ streamlined its organisation, Nic realised that he should consider semi-retirement. Pearson Education expressed interest in Nic writing *Brilliant retirement* so he started to research the subject in earnest. Nic left QinetiQ in April 2008 and now works about one day a week as a visiting research fellow at Cranfield University. In researching this book Nic has talked to hundreds of retired people. This book is their story and tells you how to recognise and avoid the many pitfalls that could spoil what should be the best part of your life. Nic has followed the advice he gives you in this book, and has an almost permanent smile on his face.

Acknowledgements

I would like to share the blame for this book with my brother Alan who encouraged me to write it in the first place, and who provided many of the key ideas.

I am indebted to Professor Marion Kloep, co-director of the Centre for Lifespan Research at the University of Glamorgan, who generously provided me with a selection of the latest research papers on retirement and aging, as well as pointing me at the seminal works of the past.

Whilst researching this book I talked to literally hundreds of people who had retired, or were about to retire. Much of the content of this book is based on the insights I obtained from these conversations. In many ways this book is their story.

When writing about financial matters it is very important to try and get your facts right. I would like to thank Martin Bamford, a chartered financial planner, who was kind enough to check the advice on investing for accuracy. Martin is a leading author on money matters and his books include *Brilliant investing, How to Retire Ten Years Early* and *The Money Tree* – all published by Prentice Hall.

Even more important is to get health issues correct. I was extremely fortunate to have the help of Dr Margaret Grant M.B., C.h.B (St Andrews), F.R.C.Anaes., F.R.C.Paeds. & C.H. Margaret graduated from St Andrews in 1968. She is a retired consultant community paediatrician in the Wyre Forest. Her special interests were neurodisability, including autistic spectrum disorders, genetics, and adoption and fostering. Margaret took a very active role in the creation of Chapter 5.

Thanks to Logan Anderson, head of customer relations at The Pensions Trust, who provided input on pensions issues.

I had the pleasure of working with two editors, Rachael Stock and then Elie Williams. I not only benefited from their professional work but I also relied on their support in seeing this book through to publication. I am also very grateful to the rest of the team at Pearson Education who have done their usual, excellent jobs.

Thanks to my wife Sue, who seems to enjoy having me around more of the time.

Introduction

This really is the golden age for retirement. At the time this book is published (2010) many people will be secure financially because they have good occupational pensions. Thanks to modern medicine, you should have a long and active life ahead of you. If you still want to do some work there are likely to be many opportunities for you. The power of the 'grey pound' is now well understood so there are lots of great products and services being targeted specifically at you. Finally, society now has a much more positive attitude to more mature, and also less able, people.

As time goes by towards 2020, people will have to work longer and, unless you follow my advice about saving for retirement, then you will have to manage with smaller retirement incomes than those who retired before 2010. However this needn't prevent you from having a brilliant retirement, so read on ...

Many people have wonderful retirements, but I found often they had faced both serious and minor problems, many of which could have been avoided. This book allows you to learn from their experiences and insights.

I started to research this book a year before starting my own retirement and finished writing it 18 months after I had retired. I talked to literally hundreds of retired people and I found an interesting paradox – almost every retired person had forged a uniquely different retired life, while at the same time everyone

I talked to raised the same issues time and again. Speaking personally I can honestly say that I have found those experiences very useful in my own transition into retirement.

I found many insights into both retirement and aging contained in the recent publications from academic researchers. This research agreed with what I learned from talking to retired people. However, the researchers also offered theories that helped explain their observations. These theories were often useful because they helped me to offer you advice on how to get the most out of your retirement. I was also very fortunate to get help from medical, financial and pensions experts.

This book contains not only a lot of relevant information, but also I have tried to 'get off the fence' and offer you opinionated advice that I believe will help you have a much more fulfilling retirement. Provided you interpret my advice to your own unique circumstances you should find this book extremely helpful.

My research identified the major issues that retired people felt I should cover, which includes:

- using your preparations for retirement to help you make an easier and better transition into retirement
- adjusting to the very real shock of retirement
- how to manage your savings, reduce your outgoings, maximise your income and other financial matters – whilst recognising when you are receiving self-serving advice from financial advisers
- how to maintain a positive state of mind, which is the key to managing your problems and staying happy
- how to enjoy the best possible health and to manage your health issues
- how to handle the strains that your retirement will place on your relationships with partners, family, friends and the rest of society

- how to maintain your independence so you can maximise the time you can continue to live in your own home.

There can be no 'one size fits all' formula, but you will be able to adapt my advice to your own unique circumstances, so that you can have a brilliant retirement. If you find the book helpful then please recommend it to friends and relatives.

CHAPTER 1

Preparing for retirement

A surprising number of people work very long hours up to the day they retire and, on the first day of their retirement, are completely unprepared for the prospect of having nothing specific to do for the rest of their lives. Many of these people go through a significant trauma in the transition to retirement. There is well-researched evidence that planning and rehearsal for a life-changing event such as retirement will reduce such trauma significantly. Preparations can be very practical, but just as important are the psychological ones.

Psychological preparations

Letting go of work

Work was such an important part of your life that it should come as no surprise that leaving it behind will be a great psychological shock. It will change your perception of who you are, and it will also change other people's perception of you. Many people also like to feel indispensable at work, and enjoy the respect and authority they have. Whilst working you may complain at the number of interruptions you have to deal with each day to sort your colleagues' problems out ... but many people miss it once it's gone. There are many techniques that you can use to prepare for these problems.

Staging retirement

It is increasingly common for people to avoid a 'big bang' retirement. You might move to a job that uses your experience but has fewer responsibilities and pressures. You may move to part-time working. You might return to work as a consultant. The options available to workers seem to be growing all the time.

Many organisations have frequent reorganisations. You can use these as opportunities to try something new, which combines a new challenge with less pressure. Alternatively, reorganisations may also be used for downsizing. A gentle hint that you might be open to an attractive offer to leave or become part-time may lead to a good outcome in the current, or a future, reorganisation.

By the time you reach your fifties it is possible that you will have ceased to climb the greasy pole and that further promotions are unlikely. You may want to consider adjusting your work/life balance, for example:

- You may decide to stop working very long hours – you may well be surprised that you get as much, or more, good quality work done in fewer hours.
- If you have a successful career, you may be committed, to the point of obsession, to your work. If you are living to work, rather than working to live, you may want to try and become less obsessed and to lighten up a bit.
- You may be very competitive, and very involved in office politics. Again, you may want to take work a little less obsessively.
- You may well be someone who frequently volunteers to take on more responsibility; should you consider letting younger colleagues take on these tasks, possibly with you as a mentor?

Succession planning

Helping to train your replacement will help you adjust positively to the reality that you are not indispensable.

Planning for new challenges

Retirement researchers talk about retirement often being driven by a mixture of 'push' forces, which are forcing you out of the workforce, and 'pull' forces where the attractions of retirement make you willing to leave voluntarily. By thinking about what will happen after you cease doing your current job full-time, you are likely to increase the pull forces. If you have strong pull forces you will be less likely to suffer from a traumatic retirement experience.

It can be very helpful to make preparation for starting on a new challenge before the transition to the next stage of your life actually happens. I was very lucky in that I got the offer to write *Brilliant retirement* before I left full-time work, and it meant that I had one goal straight away.

brilliant tip

It is worth preparing for retirement in good time – it is never too early to start your financial preparations for retirement, and once you reach 50 you may want to start thinking about psychological and practical preparations for when you eventually retire. Push forces can build up surprisingly quickly, and you don't want to be unprepared if this happens.

Start developing a new social network

A common reaction to retirement is, 'I don't miss the work, but I do miss the people.' If you have a restricted circle of friends

make new friends
before you leave your
current job

and acquaintances outside work
then you will benefit from starting to
make new friends before you leave
your current job.

Practical preparations

Potential relationship problems

If you have issues in a relationship then it is more likely that
retirement will make things worse, rather than better. The road
to hell is paved with the course of least resistance. If a relationship hits problems and you choose to see a counsellor, the most
common issue that the counsellor will highlight is the need for
greater communication. We don't tend to talk about relationship problems with partners, parents, children, other relations,
friends, etc. The solution is usually simple – talk openly about
the problem. If things are really bad, it may be best to seek
counselling sooner rather than later.

It isn't just problems you need to talk about, your retirement is
going to have a big impact on those you live with. Establishing
a new routine is going to be disruptive to your loved ones. It is
best to talk about how you can manage this disruption before
retirement actually hits you.

Relationships with those you share your home with can be
helped by some simple practical preparations. Someone I talked
to said 'buy a shed'. You will need to think about how your
home is going to accommodate you spending much more time
in it. If possible you will need your own space, so you are not
constantly under the feet of your partner, children, etc. Talk
about, think about, and do something about it before you retire
– if necessary, buy that shed.

Your loved ones and friends are likely to think that now you are
retired, you have plenty of time to help them more. You will

probably be happy to help, but this
easily can become a burden. You
need to think about how you want
to prioritise your time, so you keep
enough time for those things you

**you have only one life
and you need to live it**

value – this is not selfish, you have only one life and you need
to live it.

 brilliant   tip

Don't leave all the work on your house until you have retired.
Although you may well have more time to do DIY, remember you
will have less disposable income to sort out problems, and to
make improvements.

Lifestyle changes

It is worth thinking about whether you are considering changing your lifestyle after retirement: moving nearer to relatives,
downsizing, or other changes to your lifestyle. For example, I
have talked to two people who have spent most of their time
on a canal boat. These are such major decisions that you don't
want to make them hurriedly.

As an example, consider the issues of making the canal network
your home. The gentle, nomadic existence of life on a canal
boat is very attractive, but there are practical issues to be considered. The canal system effectively closes down during the
winter, so you have to consider what you want to do then. One
couple sold their house and bought two small rental properties, which kept them in the property market, and left them the
option of moving back into their own house at a later date. The
rental properties also provided a useful source of income. They
moored in Birmingham during the winters and got part-time

jobs. Another couple rented out their house during the summer and moved back each winter.

Of the people I talked to there were many more who commented on missed opportunities than who said they had made a major decision they later regretted. Of those few people who regretted a major upheaval, most commented that some basic research would have warned them that they were making a mistake.

Activities

Don't wait until you have retired to think about, and prepare for, your post-retirement projects. Just like writing a book, it can be very difficult to start a project – writing the first word of a book can be very hard indeed. You will spare yourself this pressure if you have made even a modest start.

Health

Most of the suggestions I make about health in Chapter 5 are likely to be implemented when you have more time, after you retire. The one recommendation I would make is that you get your blood pressure and cholesterol checked well before you retire. When I first started work in the late 1970s, lots of people seemed to drop dead of a heart attack in their first year of retirement, especially those who were workaholics. This is much less marked now, and my suspicion is that this is because high blood pressure and high cholesterol are now much more likely to be diagnosed and treated before people retire. If you have slipped through the net, please get yourself checked now. If you are a workaholic then please read this chapter very carefully; it just might save your life. If you know a workaholic then buy them a copy of this book for Christmas!

Maintaining your independence

The internet is a godsend when it comes to maintaining your independence by supporting hobbies, communication, shopping, research, managing your finances, etc. If you aren't yet computer literate then I strongly urge you to get yourself equipped, in knowledge and facilities, as soon as possible. You should also sort out other technology issues, such as mobile phones, digital cameras, etc. ready for your retirement.

Transport is key, and many people wished they had thought about their cars well before they retired. Do you need a bigger second car, given that you intend to go down to just one car after you retire? Should you have bought something practical and cheap to run rather than another boy's toy?

transport is key

 brilliant tip

If you don't drive then, unless there is a very good reason not to, make learning to drive your first project after you retire.

Should you invest in making your house easier to maintain? Should you invest in making your house cheaper to run – for example more insulation, solar panels or a heat pump? Should you consider future mobility issues when buying or improving your house – for example checking the suitability for a chair lift, fitting a downstairs toilet or shower room, and the like?

Have you developed good, long-term relationships with professionals you may well need as you get older? These might include:

- plumbers
- electricians

- decorators
- builders and odd-job men
- cleaners
- doctors
- dentists
- osteopaths or chiropractors etc.

 **tip**

If possible, avoid rows with people. If you are not speaking to
friends, relations and trades people, then ultimately you have fewer
people to talk to, and fewer people who may be willing to help you.

Financial preparations – pensions!

You will find comprehensive coverage of financial matters in
Chapter 3 so it makes sense to defer a discussion of pensions to
the end of that chapter.

 **tip**

Try living on your retirement income before you actually retire.
Expenditure tends to expand to consume most of your disposable
income, so you will probably have to adjust your spending habits so
that you don't exceed your income after retirement.

CHAPTER 2

Adjusting to retirement

An often-quoted 'fact' is that the three most traumatic events in a person's life are a death in the family, divorce and moving house. I suspect this 'fact' was invented to highlight how stressful moving house can be. I think that the early stages of retirement can be as traumatic as any of these three events. By analysing the underlying factors that make retirement so much of an upheaval, you will understand what is happening to you and be better able to manage any problems you encounter.

I have been asked a number of times if the shock of retirement can harm your health. There have been numerous research studies into the effects of retirement on health and mortality, but unfortunately these studies report widely differing conclusions – from some saying health improves after retirement, to others saying that retirement causes significant health problems! I think it is reasonable to assume that minimising the shock of retirement can only benefit your health.

> minimising the shock of retirement can only benefit your health

An interesting and optimistic piece of research by a leading academic in the UK found from an experimental sample that many of the people who reported serious problems adjusting to retirement were those who had not been happy at work.

She theorised that many of these individuals had underlying personality issues that were the root cause of their problems. Stripping these people out of the sample, only 10 per cent of the remaining people had failed to eventually make a successful adjustment to retirement. However, many people are taken by surprise by how significantly they are affected by retirement. In the rest of this chapter I will analyse why retirement has such an impact on people, and will describe techniques that will allow you to better adjust to retirement.

What will I do with my time?

I define retirement as starting when you cease to work at the same intensity, duration, or stress levels as you had done earlier in your career. This will make time, possibly a lot of time, in your life, which needs to be filled. How are you going to fill it?

Retired people use their time in many different ways, and it is very helpful to understand the different calls on your time now you are retired.

Continue working

Many retired people want to continue, at least part time, with a regular paid, or voluntary, work commitment. The range of work commitments I encountered was vast. To illustrate the variety I will list a few:

- Part-time work for your previous employer.
- Consultancy work in your previous profession.
- Teaching/tutoring, either paid or voluntary.
- Good works – two particular examples came up time and again, which were charity and church work. Other examples include being a school governor or getting involved in local or national politics.

- Starting up a business.

- Taking on a full- or part-time job in a completely new area of business, often one that is much less high pressure than your previous profession.

Many people viewed continued working as a phase, which would decrease with time – although a few never wanted to stop.

brilliant tip

Your attitudes to retirement will probably evolve as you get older. You need to interpret the advice in this book appropriately for your current position. For example, when reading the chapter on financial issues you may find that your appetite for risk declines as you get older.

Many benefits can flow from working in retirement:

- If you are being paid, this can help if finances are tight, or purchase treats if you are already financially comfortable.

- Work is a valuable part of someone's persona. Losing your professional persona can be a big shock for people. Working in retirement can maintain your existing professional self-image or generate a new one.

> work is a valuable part of someone's persona

- Work can give someone meaning to their life. For example, many people doing voluntary work wanted to put something back into society.

- Work is often a key source of social contacts that people miss when they retire.

- Work is often the single largest part of the structure in someone's life. Losing all work structure can disturb a lot of people. Some people said that they liked to be forced to get up and go to work, and worried that the pace of life would slow too much if they gave up work altogether.

● Work used to fill a large part of your time and you may appreciate the time it can still occupy in your life.

brilliant tip

If you are giving up work then you need to think about handling the loss of your professional persona, social network and the structure to your days. You need to find replacements for what you have lost, for example by consciously making time to maintain a social network.

Fulfilling an ambition

You now have the time to fulfil some of your ambitions. Examples that people told me about included:

● Learn to play the piano.

● Bicycle to Italy.

● Write a book.

● Research a family tree.

● Study a particular subject.

● Get a degree.

● Join the University of the Third Age (U3A).

● Restore a classic car.

● Learn to ride a motor bike.

● Visit a particular, far-off country.

● Learn to speak French.

● Learn to fly a plane.

Tackling projects

Less lofty than your ambitions, there are likely to be a number of projects you have always wanted to tackle. Examples might be:

● Sort out your toolshed.

● File/digitise your photographs.

● Write a piece of software.

● Learn to use a computer.

● Create the perfect lawn (that one's mine).

● Create a vegetable patch.

● Tackle a DIY project (or 20!).

Counting wasps

A retired neighbour asked another neighbour, 'Are you getting many wasps this year?' The exasperated answer from the young working mother was, 'I don't have time to count wasps!' There are so many things you now have time for. Some common examples I have heard include:

> there are so many things you now have time for

● See more of your grandchildren, friends and relatives.

● Sleep in if you want to.

● Read the newspaper properly.

● Read the pile of books you have bought over the years.

● Go off for days out or spontaneous weekends away.

● Spend more time on a hobby.

I leave you the pleasure of completing your own list.

 **fact**

The word most commonly used by retired people to researchers to sum up retirement is 'freedom'.

 **tip**

Beware that counting wasps can fill your time so completely that you never get onto your projects and ambitions.

Freedom – I don't have to ...

I highlighted in the last section the freedom you have as a retired person to do what you want to do. A delightful flipside of this freedom, which will come as a shock to the system, is the number of things you no longer have to do, which used to dominate your life:

- Get up at a particular time.
- Dress in your work clothes.
- Commute to and from work.
- Face the relentless pressures of work deadlines.
- Deal with office politics.
- Shop and do all your chores over the weekend, while trying to unwind.

This sounds marvellous; it is marvellous. However, the structure of your old life has disappeared. Indeed, you are now a new person in your own eyes and in the eyes of your friends, relatives and the rest of society. You need new strategies to adjust to your new life.

Some adjustment strategies

Establish a new routine

Total freedom is too much like anarchy for most retired people. The key phase in the early stages of retirement is to establish a new routine. On the first day of your retirement it is very easy to think that you are now on holiday for the rest of your life. Most people I talked to had realised that a never-ending holiday would soon pall, however they also soon appreciated

don't be a slave to your routine

that you should not establish such a rigid routine that you didn't enjoy your new freedoms. A constant warning I heard was the danger as you get older of becoming a slave to your routine.

> **brilliant** tip
>
> Just because normally you do something at a fixed time is no reason not to do something else if you prefer.

A routine is something very practical and tangible that can help you adjust to retirement. The next point is just as important, but much less tangible.

Establish a new persona

For many working people their job is a very large part of who they think they are – 'I am a doctor/teacher/solicitor, (etc.)'. Losing this identity can come as a big shock. This is especially true for men, and more so for high-achieving men. Women often have a leading role in the home, even if they have high-powered professional lives, and after retirement they have this home-based role to fall back on. Even someone who isn't overtly status-conscious can be quite disturbed when they lose their work status. In addition, many people have significant power over others in their working lives, and losing that power can be very disturbing. As discussed previously, some retired people will develop a new persona by continuing to work in a paid or voluntary capacity. At the other extreme, you may present yourself as, 'I am retired, and I don't know how I found the time to go to work'. Most people will benefit from consciously thinking about how they wish to describe their new identity.

Wean yourself off adrenaline

Most workers are 'adrenaline junkies', where the constant stream of deadlines, crises and travel used to provide the buzz to keep going. For some people the withdrawal symptoms can be quite unpleasant. Improving your diet and taking more exercise definitely seems to help. Throwing yourself into a pet project can also be a good tactic. Starting your retirement with a long holiday has worked well for some people. The main point of this section is that by recognising the problem you are already a long way towards solving it.

Develop your social network

When you leave work you will lose a major source of social contact with friends and colleagues. I strongly advise you to invest time in building up a replacement network of friends. There are many ways of doing this:

- You can make the effort to talk to people – on the bus, at the gym, over the garden fence, etc.
- You can spend time meeting up with neighbours, friends, former colleagues, relatives, and the like.

- You can take up social activities such as walking, swimming, The University of The Third Age, hobbies, etc.
- You can throw parties.

 **tip**

If you have a partner it can be very easy to overly rely on them for social intercourse. If anything happens to your partner this can leave you very vulnerable to loneliness. You both need to have shared friends, but you also need your own individual friends.

Read the rest of the book

Future chapters will address other key adjustment techniques. These include how to manage your health and finances and how your relationships with partners, relatives and friends need to be managed.

CHAPTER 3

Money
matters

The subject that often causes retired people the most angst is money. There are a number of reasons for this. First and foremost is the concern about whether you will be able to live on a reduced income, and whether you can protect that income and your savings from the ravages of inflation. Another big concern is people's belief that they do not understand money matters, and they find it very hard to get skilled, impartial financial advice. People realise that with their main source of income gone, they will find it very hard, or impossible, to recover from financial mistakes – savings once gone probably will never be replenished. They are often very worried about taking financial risks – a number of people lose sleep worrying about whether their investments are safe. Lastly, people worry because they do not know how long they will live, and hence find it hard to plan for their old age. This chapter will help you tackle all these issues and, having read it, you will be much better placed to manage your finances. Let's start by discussing the issues you will face in the early days of your retirement.

Adjusting to retirement

Even if you are one of the fortunate people to have a decent occupational pension, and to have a reasonable amount of savings, the chances are that your retirement income is going to be a substantial drop from what you have been used to. Most of the people I talked to were worried about how they would cope. Thankfully, because they were worried, they became much more aware of financial issues, and hence adjusted to their new circumstances very successfully.

Having done my best to worry you, I can reassure you that things are almost certainly not as bad as you fear. The difference between your current income and your previous income,

> things are almost certainly not as bad as you fear

may have been taxed at a high rate so your disposable income drops much less than you might think. For example, in my own case I was paying nearly 50% tax (both income tax and National Insurance) on that difference. You will also probably find that many expenses are much less; areas you are likely to make savings include:

- travel costs of commuting
- cars – do you need two cars? Do you need an expensive car? Do you need to change it frequently? Do you need to buy new cars or can you buy second-hand?
- smart work clothes
- money you used to spend to save time – ready meals, takeaways, help to do jobs around the home and garden that now you can do yourself.

Managing your spending

The best person to open this section is Charles Dickens with his Micawber principle from *David Copperfield*:

Annual income twenty pounds, annual expenditure nineteen nineteen and six, result happiness. Annual income twenty pounds, annual expenditure twenty pounds nought and six, result misery.

What can you learn from the Micawber principle? If you, and your partner (if you have one), are not good with money, it is best to

it is best to set yourself a budget

set yourself a budget. Even if you are very comfortably off then you will probably want to use some, or many, of the techniques from this section.

brilliant tip

Almost every retired person I talked to said it is virtually impossible to predict how comfortably off (or how hard up) you will be until you have been retired for over a year. Almost everyone advised that you be cautious with your spending for at least the first year of retirement.

Your expenditure divides into two basic classes – essential and discretionary. We might argue what exactly is in each class, but you will probably agree that the following are essential:

- taxes
- household bills (electricity, gas, water, telephone/internet)
- clothes
- food
- household goods (washing powder, etc.)
- insurance
- household appliances
- building maintenance.

Discretionary expenditure items include:

- foreign holidays
- toys for boys (the latest electronic gadgets, etc.)
- entertainment (theatre, cinema, the pub, restaurants ...)

- frequent changes of car
- paintings and other decorative items.

 **tip**

Prioritise your discretionary expenditure so you can protect the things you get greatest pleasure from.

Major savings are possible by curbing your discretionary expenditure and intelligently shopping/negotiating for the essentials. As an example, your weekly spend at supermarkets can be reduced easily by 30% (or more) if you do not currently shop in multiple supermarkets for special offers and reduced items, and if you do not make efforts to reduce waste. Likewise, by shopping around for energy providers and insurance you can make useful savings for just a few hours' effort. Haggling for larger purchases again can deliver substantial savings (buy my book *Brilliant negotiations* if you are not a born haggler – which will also help my retirement income!).

Now you are retired you have time to make your money go further – many retired people make a hobby of bargain hunting, and get a lot of pleasure from bagging a great bargain.

 **tip**

When shopping around for insurance you may want to avoid constantly changing your car insurer. As you get older it is often worth building up a long-term relationship with a reputable insurer, because you do not want your insurer to withdraw insurance cover when you become elderly.

The potential savings on your discretionary expenditure will be very large indeed. This is one reason why it can be worth doing at least one budget – you will be shocked by how much some items cost you. You will probably find that items such as cars, wine, expensive holidays, eating out and take-aways have been swallowing a substantial part of your income. Remember the Micawber principle, and be prepared to cut your expenditure to fit your new income. One reason for shopping wisely is to leave more room for discretionary expenditure.

 **example**

When my wife and I did a budget we were stunned by how much we spent on alcohol. We drank a bottle of wine most nights, and we found our average spend was £8 per bottle. When we had parties we liked to buy expensive wine for our guests. Add in the sherry, spirits and the like and we were spending about £4,000 a year. Since retiring we drink about a third less (as part of our healthy-living drive), and now shop almost exclusively for half-price offers, which we combine with case discounts and promotional coupons. We now spend approximately £1,500 p.a., and enjoy our booze every bit as much as we did before.

Generating earned income

Many people supplement their pensions and unearned income by part-time work. As I explained in Chapter 2 there are many non-financial benefits to continued work, but in this chapter I should certainly mention that the money you earn can be an important supplement to your income. As the years go by it is likely that many people will find themselves retiring with less generous occupational pensions, and the need to keep working part-time probably will increase.

I would like to highlight one particular situation where it is possible for retired people to have problems. Some retired people decide to start their own business; if you decide to follow this route then I have a few words of caution.

First off, you must think very carefully before risking a substantial part of your savings on a business venture. I strongly recommend that you do a detailed analysis of what you might lose in the worst-case scenario, and then decide if you can really afford this risk. Then you must ensure that you monitor your finances and don't end up losing even more – it is much better to close a business than continue pouring good money after bad.

Even if you have modest aspirations and are not risking a lot of money, you will still want your business to be a success. I strongly recommend you take a professional approach to any business venture. I used to be in the difficult position where there was no book on start-ups that I was comfortable to recommend. I am happy to say there is now such a book, and I am even more pleased to say it is in the *Brilliant* series. It is called *Brilliant start-up* by Caspian Woods.

You must not ignore the tax, legal and regulatory implications of any business. Find out what you must do, talk to the tax authorities, take out any necessary insurance – it pays to be careful or, more accurately, it can cost you dear to be careless.

Financial planning

I think, for good reasons, this book is very upbeat about the excellent prospects you have for a great retirement. I have not dwelt on the sombre subjects of death, incapacity and other disasters. When it comes to your financial affairs you are, in my opinion, being negligent if you do not consider these issues in good time.

Make a will

There is an apocryphal story that at a solicitor's dinner they drink two toasts; the first is to those who do not make a will, and the second is to those who make their own will. Yes, it is very uncomfortable thinking about what happens to your money and possessions after you die, but the misery it will cause if you do not make a will really makes it essential that you grasp this nettle. I would strongly advise you seek professional advice in drawing up your will, because you are likely to miss a number of key issues, and wills need to be properly drafted.

> wills need to be properly drafted

 **brilliant**   tip

Having made a will you need to keep it up to date.

Set up a power of attorney

In many countries you can set up a legal agreement for someone else to manage your affairs if you become incapacitated. It can be a nightmare for those trying to care for you if you have not set up in advance what the UK calls a power of attorney (property and affairs). I strongly recommend that you do so.

They say that the only certain things in life are death and taxes, so I will now discuss tax planning – starting with the tax on death.

> the only certain things in life are death and taxes

Manage any inheritance tax liabilities

Do you really want the Government to get its hands on your money after you die? Some countries have done away with this iniquitous tax, but others still levy it. If your estate is likely to be subject to inheritance tax then either research the subject carefully or, better still, seek competent professional advice.

At the same time you can also think about whether you want to pass some of your money on to your children, grandchildren, nieces, nephews, etc. before you die.

Minimising your tax liability

If you are married or are in a civil partnership, then both partners will get an allowance of income that is tax-free. Also, if either partner is paying higher-rate tax and the other is not, then it pays to transfer assets to whoever pays the least income tax.

Similarly, most countries tax the gains you make on capital, especially shares. Many people have unbalanced investment portfolios where some large items would attract significant capital gains tax (CGT) if they were sold. Most countries have an allowance that allows some gains to be taken tax-free. It makes sense to transfer assets between partners so that the CGT allowance of both partners is used to the full when rebalancing your portfolio, or when taking gains to supplement your income.

Most countries have some tax-free savings schemes. In the UK there are individual savings accounts (ISAs). ISAs provide a shelter from CGT, provide a limit on the amount of income tax you pay on shares, unit trusts and investment trusts, and also provide income tax-free for bonds (which are discussed later), or for limited sums in savings accounts. These schemes are usually worth taking full advantage of. Likewise, many countries have tax-free investment products – in the UK they are mostly under the banner of NS&I or premium bonds. High-rate tax-payers may well find these attractive, and even standard-rate taxpayers may find the rates acceptable given they are mostly zero-risk investments. However, a word of warning – do not get so carried away by the tax saving that you override your strategic approach to the balance of risk in your investment portfolio.

Pay for appropriate insurance

Do not skimp on the protection you get for property, house contents, holiday, car and other forms of insurance. By all means shop around for the best deals, but make sure you are covered properly by reputable insurance companies. For travel insurance you may need to find an insurer that specialises in cover for more mature travellers.

Managing your savings

When preparing to write this book I thought I would simply advise you to find a good independent financial adviser (IFA) and follow their advice. How naïve could I be? Your problem is that in some countries (including the UK) financial advisers get most of their income from commissions on the financial products they sell. Those investments that I believe will be best for you offer no commissions, so are seldom if ever recommended. In addition, even within a particular class of products such as guaranteed equity bonds, or unit trusts, commissions are often highest on products that are less attractive than those offering lower commissions. Even worse, or in my opinion much worse, are those financial advisers who are not labelled as independent, for example so-called personal bank managers and financial advisers of banks and building societies, who are little more than salesmen for their bank's products.

The very best IFAs will work for fees and will refund commissions, but regrettably the whole market is so dominated by commission-bearing products that often you will still get less than optimal advice. In addition, commissions are substantial, and often use management charges to pay the IFAs annually for products they have sold in the past (so-called trail commissions). As a consequence, IFAs usually will make more money out of commissions than by working on a fee-only basis, and hence some IFAs tend not to be very motivated when working for fees. It is best to choose a financial adviser who openly advertises that they will work for fees. If an IFA is not totally open about commissions I urge you strongly to go elsewhere for advice. I also urge you strongly to ask your adviser about commissions and, unless the answer is clear and acceptable, again you will do best to go elsewhere.

 **tip**

There are a number of reputable discount stockbrokers who refund the bulk of up-front commissions on investment products such as unit trusts. I happily use such a stockbroker, and can think of no good reason to pay commissions unnecessarily.

There are a range of qualifications that indicate how much formal training an IFA has undergone. The minimum qualifications to advertise yourself as an IFA are very basic indeed. If an IFA has only a Certificate in Financial Planning, then they have not invested heavily in their own qualifications. The next levels up are the Diploma or Advanced Diploma in Financial Planning (formerly called the Advanced Financial Planning Certificate). The top qualifications are the Chartered Financial Planner and Certified Financial Planner qualifications. As is so often the case, you get what you pay for! Regardless of qualifications I suggest you ask some questions based on the contents of this chapter. For example, you might ask for a comparison of unit and investment trusts. Likewise, you might ask for a simple explanation of bonds. If you do not find the answers clear, accurate and jargon-free then just walk away.

At the top end of the market, there are wealth consultants from stockbrokers and prestige banks, who charge very significant fees, usually based on a percentage of the value of your savings that they manage. I suspect that some of these are very good. Again you need to check that they are not also collecting commissions on the products they recommend. This chapter will arm you with enough knowledge to be able to evaluate their advice.

As a final word of warning, you need to know that financial advisers have hardly ever been successfully sued, even when their advice has been reckless, incompetent or negligent. Some professionals, such as doctors, have to be very careful about their advice because there is a major risk of being sued for negligence; financial advisers do not have to be anywhere near so careful when helping you to look after a lifetime of savings.

My comments about financial advisers are correct at the time of writing, but the Financial Services Agency (FSA) in the UK has been considering reform of the legislation covering financial advisers for some considerable time. It is quite likely that they will grasp the nettle and force the top tier of IFAs to be funded totally by fees rather than commission. If the FSA implement such a reform it will become vastly easier to get truly impartial, expert financial advice.

 tip

As is so often true in this life, the best way to locate a good financial adviser is by personal recommendation.

This sounds bad, but I am afraid it gets worse. The financial press, for example in newspapers, sometimes tacitly toes the IFA's line by not pointing out commission-free or low-commission products. In addition the financial press can be very faddish, often

the financial press can
be very faddish

highlighting investment areas that are near the top of their financial cycles, whereas an investor usually will do better to buy into less fashionable areas. This is not to say that all the comment and advice in the financial press is bad, indeed I have found many gems – but, as the princess said, 'I had to kiss a lot of frogs first.'

My advice is that you have to learn enough about investing to manage your investments yourself, and to treat any advice you read in the press or decide to pay for, as just that – advice. The good news is that it is not rocket science, and you can now read on for an elementary description of how to build rockets.

brilliant tip

Read the money/business sections of your newspaper every day. Although it will contain a lot of faddish and dangerous advice, it will also contain many useful facts and a lot of sound advice. Once you understand financial matters quite well you will be able to spot, and benefit from, the good advice. It will also help you develop your financial knowledge.

Inflation – a dominant factor

Protecting your investments from the ravages of inflation is likely to be a dominant factor in your investment strategy.

brilliant fact

If inflation stayed at a low figure of just 2.5% over a 10-year period then £50,000 would be worth only £38,800 at the end of the 10-year period. Obviously if inflation increases significantly above 2.5% the figures get far worse.

Putting your savings into low-risk investments such as government-backed savings products or the best savings accounts from banks and building societies will yield only a small percentage above inflation. So, if you need to live on the income from your investments, the low-risk option in real terms will mean you are eating into your savings and your income will decline as you get older. With increasing life expectancies most retired people would be well advised to plan to maintain a decent standard of living into their 80s. This means that most retired people have to invest for the long term and there is no truly safe option to managing your investments.

brilliant tip

As you get older your savings have to last for fewer years, and you may find you are less comfortable taking risks and expending effort actively managing your investments. Consequently, you may want to readjust your investment portfolio so that it becomes lower risk.

Your attitude to risk

You have to decide how much risk you are willing to take. This chapter gives you a significant number of facts that will help you decide what approach to take. It is advisable that you get your finances ready for retirement well in advance, and if you have done so you will have got used to fluctuations in the value of your portfolio over a number of years.

brilliant tip

There is a wide range of investment products, called structured products, that play on people's fears about losing their investments. For example, there are products called guaranteed equity bonds, which pay a percentage of the gains in the stock market over a fixed period of years, but give you your investment stake back if the stock market goes down. You would be wise to avoid all such products. For example, guaranteed equity bond providers keep the income from investments and, as you will see, income from equities is very important indeed. There is a saying that 'you don't get something for nothing', and you will pay a very high price for any protection provided. These products usually pay financial advisers big commissions, so they tend to be sold hard.

Everyone knows that you should not have all your eggs in one basket, and this sound advice is at the heart of any well-designed investment portfolio. It is also worth remembering that some of your investments will do better than others and what started out as a well-balanced portfolio can, after a number of years, become unbalanced. This means that you need to review the structure of your portfolio on a regular basis.

Structuring your portfolio

The advice published by the stockbrokers and independent financial advisers Hargreaves Lansdown in May 2008 about a possible structure for portfolios is as follows:

For a high-income portfolio they suggest:

- 50% in UK Equity Income unit and investment trusts
- 10% in non-UK Equity Income
- 30% in the safest (Investment-Grade) Corporate Bonds
- 10% in riskier high-yield Corporate Bonds.

The portfolio would be for your investments after you have set aside a suitable safety net in readily accessible, high-interest, cash savings.

For a balanced income and growth portfolio they suggest:

- 80% in UK Equity Income
- 10% in UK Growth
- 10% in non-UK Equity Income.

In my opinion the balanced income and growth portfolio would be the basis for a very decent high-growth portfolio if all the income was reinvested.

These are only guidelines, and other stockbrokers and IFAs will have their own ideas, but I thought it worth mentioning this advice because I suspect many readers will be very surprised by the high percentage that they suggest investing in the stock market in unit and investment trusts. I believe that this approach is sound advice – as you will see from the rest of this chapter.

 **fact**

The figure I find most interesting is that £100 invested in the stock market in 1899 on average will have increased to £213 if you took the income each year, but if you reinvested the income it will have grown to £25,022. Whereas £100 of government bonds (gilts) will have dropped to just one pound in value, and reinvesting income will have yielded only £323 after inflation is taken into account.

What about property I hear you ask? Over the 25 years up to 2008, house prices grew by 507% whereas the equity market's value grew by 1,914%. Many people trust property because you can see it and touch it, but you should remember that a country's stock market represents a very large proportion of the national wealth, so it is underpinned by something of great tangible value. Many people also have a much rosier view of rises in house prices than is warranted. For example, from the peak of the property market in the UK in 1989 it wasn't until 2002 that house prices had recovered in real terms (including the effects of inflation).

Unfortunately the rise of the hedge funds in the twenty-first century has increased stock market volatility, but if the stock market does not continue to grow at historical rates over the long term then your country is in big trouble.

Having decided your basic strategy and appetite for risk, the next questions you face are what to buy and when to buy it?

What to buy?

The stock market – shares

If you want to invest in the stock market and to generate both growth and a high income from that investment, there are basically three ways to do it:

1   Buy individual shares with high yields. The remaining two options are collective investments where your money (and the money of many other investors) is invested in a basket of high-yielding shares (and occasionally bonds/gilts as well).

2   Unit trusts and open-ended investment companies (OEICs).

3   Investment trusts.

Individual shares are for enthusiasts and for well-off people who are paying for expert advice. Alternatively, if you are well off, you easily can research the 40 plus shares that dominate the portfolios of high-income unit trusts, OEICs and investment trusts, and buy those. It would be interesting to know if what you lose by not actively managing your portfolio is more or less than you gain from saving the costs associated with unit trusts, OEICS and investment trusts.

I have lumped unit trusts and OEICs together because I believe they are little different. OEICs have the advantage that they do not have separate prices for buying and selling, which typically is an extra 5% that you lose when you buy/sell unit trusts. There are other technical differences but I do not believe that they are very significant.

 brilliant   definition

An investment trust is a company whose assets are other investments – shares, bonds, cash etc.

Comparing unit trusts and investment trusts shows that investment trusts are a clear winner. Choosing investment trusts over unit trusts has many advantages:

> investment trusts are a clear winner

- Annual management costs are significantly lower, partly because investment trusts do not pay annual commissions to people who sell their products.

- There are no initial charges when purchasing the products, which typically can be 5%.

- There is a single buying/selling price, whereas typically you get 5% less when you sell a unit trust than when you buy it. Again this is because investment trusts do not pay commissions to sellers of their products.

- Unit trusts are more heavily regulated, which gives investment trusts more flexibility to take advantage of buying and selling opportunities. As an example, investment funds can build up large cash reserves, or borrow, to take advantage of the transitions between bear (falling) and bull (rising) markets.

- Unit trusts have to sell shares when there are many sellers of their unit trusts. Likewise they have to buy shares when many people buy into the unit trusts. As people tend to buy and sell in large numbers at exactly the wrong time, this can be a significant problem. As an example, unit trusts that invest in corporate bonds go up in value at a time when it is usually too late to buy such bonds advantageously.

● Investment trusts are often valued at a discount. A discount is when the value of the shares that an investment trust owns, less any borrowings, is greater than the sum of the value of all its shares (the investment trust's market capitalisation). A substantial discount is seen by many investors as an indication that an investment trust offers good value.

 **fact**

The statistics support my view that investment trusts are better than unit trusts. Over 10 years up to 2008 the average investment trust returned £246 on a £100 investment, whereas the average unit trust returned £183.

There is a view amongst many analysts that the freedom to borrow makes investment trusts riskier than unit trusts. This can, however, be offset when an investment trust trades at a discount. In addition unit trust managers are under huge pressure to get to the top of the unit trusts' performance league tables. When I researched the holdings of the best performing high-income equity unit trusts I found that their portfolios were often heavily biased towards individual sectors. For example, one had its two top holdings in tobacco companies, whilst another had its top two investments in oil companies. In contrast, all the high-income investment trusts I researched had well-balanced portfolios.

In addition to high-income investment trusts, those investment trusts that specialise in small companies usually offer high returns. This can be a useful source of diversification within a portfolio.

 **tip**

Having praised investment trusts I should warn you to avoid so-called 'split caps'. These split an investment trust into two parts: one getting most of the capital gains, and the other getting most of the income. Historically split caps have not performed as well as standard high-income equity investment trusts.

Bonds

 definition

Bonds are when you lend the government, a company or other organisation, an amount of money, for a fixed period of time, at a fixed rate of interest. At the end of the period, unless the company has gone bust and defaulted on its bonds, you get your money back. Bonds usually pay interest once or twice a year.

Some bonds (e.g. from banks and building societies) can be redeemed early and you will lose part of your interest. Bonds from government (called gilts) and corporate bonds can be bought and sold on the open market and, like shares, their values can go up and down over time.

There are two main reasons why bond prices go up and down:

1 If you buy a bond that is yielding 5% and then your central bank reduces interest rates by 1% then your bond usually will increase in value so that its effective yield is roughly 4%. Likewise if the central bank rate increases then your bond usually will drop in value.

2 Bonds in companies that are more likely to go bust, and hence default on their bonds, are worth less than the bonds

of more solid companies, which are less likely to go bust. This is the reason why very safe gilts pay less interest than corporate bonds. If a company hits trouble and the major credit rating companies (Moodys and Standard & Poor (S&P)) reduce their credit ratings, then its bonds usually will decrease in value. Likewise if a company stages a recovery and its credit rating goes up, then its bonds probably will increase in value.

 brilliant definition

The top-end bonds, in terms of safety, are called *investment grade* bonds. The bottom end bonds are called *junk* bonds. I would not get hung up on these titles, and would make your own assessment of whether a company is likely to go bust. Both Moodys and S&P have websites that allow you to register to see companies' credit ratings, which may assist your judgement.

Bonds are the safest form of investment in companies. Even if shares are nearly worthless, a company will often recover, or will be taken over, in which case it will not default on its bonds. Ignoring junk bonds, default rates measured as a percentage are historically in the low single figures. In my view, unless you are a very nervous investor then corporate bonds are a better bet than gilts – provided you do not have too much money in any one bond.

bonds are the safest form of investment in companies

It is surprisingly difficult to buy individual bonds, and many stockbrokers will recommend you buy a unit trust that specialises in bonds. Unit trusts specialising in bonds are not bad investments if you buy them at the right time of the market cycle, but personally I prefer to cut out the costs of the middle men and make the effort to buy individual bonds, just as the best wealth managers do for their clients. If you insist, then any reputable stockbroker will buy them for you, and many will have the facility to hold them in an ISA or self-invested pension plan (SIPP) for you. To get all the data on bonds in the UK either ask your stockbroker for the data or (in the UK) use the excellent website www.bondscape.co.uk, which provides a link to the previous day's closing prices, together with all the key data you will need to choose bonds. You need to remember that corporate bonds pay their income gross (no tax deducted), so unless you have them in a tax-free wrapper such as an ISA or SIPP, you will need to declare them on your income tax return.

You also need to be aware that if you buy a corporate bond then the purchase price will be higher than the selling price. As most investors intend to hold bonds for a very long time this usually is not a big problem.

 **brilliant**   definition

Yield: One of the nice things about bonds is that they are really quite easy to understand. There is only one complication that is worth understanding. There are two ways of measuring what percentage interest a bond yields. The *current yield* is the percentage yield you get in the years before maturity. However, when the bond matures you will make either a gain or loss depending on whether the price you paid was more or less than the issue price of the bond. The *yield to maturity* takes this gain/loss into account.

 **tip**

In the UK, if you invest in corporate bonds, or a unit trust that specialises in bonds, within an individual savings account (ISA) then your interest is tax-free (or it was at the time this book was written).

Property

The simplest way to make money from property is to rent out a room (or rooms) or flat in your home. Often it can be worth investing in some modifications to your house to create a separate apartment. The major downside is that this can be quite disruptive, but some people find the disruption tolerable, or indeed may welcome it – for example, if they live on their own. You will want to research (using the internet or by buying an appropriate book) the known pitfalls of renting out part of your home before you embark on this course of action; but the amount of money you can generate can be substantial.

You can downsize to a smaller house and invest the proceeds. Alternatively, you can do an equity release deal to free up capital from your property. You will want to research the issues relating to equity release before doing such a deal – for example, to ensure there are no problems if you want to move house later. However, most equity release deals allow you to free up a portion of your house's value, with interest payable only after your death, which usually will be capped to the value of your house at your death. There is an organisation that self-regulates the industry called the Safe Home Income Plans, and their website may be helpful – www.ship-ltd.org. The amount you can release depends on your age – with typical figures at the time of writing being as follows:

Age	Maximum loan to value %	Maximum loan
55	23	£57,500
60	28	£70,000
65	33	£82,500
70	38	£95,000
75	41.5	£103,750

At the time of writing most equity release schemes seem to be a fair balance between the lender and yourself.

 **brilliant** tip

If you are entitled to government support, such as pension credit, then equity release will increase your savings so you will probably no longer be eligible.

You can invest your savings, or use savings plus a mortgage, to buy a property that you will rent out. Again you will want to research the issues involved *very* carefully. You will want to check that the *net* return (both income and potential capital growth) is acceptable and warrants the risk, worry and effort of renting out. As you are now retired you may well feel you have the time to devote to what can be a time-consuming business venture. Obviously, life will be easier if the property is local to you and you are skilled at DIY for when maintenance problems arise. Some people combine such ventures with the purchase of a holiday home – and yet again you should thoroughly research the potential problems before attempting this. The potential capital growth will be very dependent on the timing of your purchase, and this will be discussed in the later section *Get your timing right.*

Remember that owning a rental property involves major financial risks. Just a few examples include:

- A collapse in house prices and great difficulty finding a buyer if you need to sell.
- Subsidence.
- Other major structural problems in a wholly owned or shared development.
- Environmental disasters such as floods and storms.
- Developments in the locality (new road, airport, sewer works, nuclear power station, power lines, wind farm, etc.).
- The neighbourhood's desirability deteriorating.
- Tenants trashing the property, and other 'bad tenant' problems.
- Squatters.
- Local laws and market conditions if you purchase abroad.
- A major decline in the number of people renting in your property's locality, or a sudden increase in other rental properties.

You can also buy a range of shares that are based on property. There are unit trusts, a few investment trusts, and also some major companies that own and rent out commercial properties, many of which pay substantial dividends. As with all property and equity investments, timing is crucial and these will be discussed in the *Get your timing right* section. It is, however, worth remembering that if you own your own home you probably already have an investment portfolio dominated by property.

Get your timing right

Probably the most difficult problem the private investor faces is knowing when to buy, or when not to buy, investments. For example if you put a large lump sum into the stock market just before the dot com bubble burst in 2000, it was 2007 before the FTSE had recovered. If you had put that lump sum into technology stocks you might well never see your money back. Earlier in this chapter I have given some even more frightening figures about how long the property market can take to recover after a housing bubble bursts.

There are some techniques that help regular investors to minimise these problems, plus you can learn from history and be aware of indicators that will help you decide if the time is right to invest a lump sum in a particular investment.

Pound cost averaging

This is just a posh phrase for saying that you should drip feed your money at regular intervals into an investment. Most reputable financial advisers recommend pound cost averaging for regular saving into the stock market. There is, however, less agreement as to whether you should drip feed a cash lump sum into the stock market or

> pound cost averaging seems to be the safest bet

take the risk and get into the market quickly – which is where historical indicators may help. If in doubt, pound cost averaging seems to me to be the safest bet.

Price to earning ratio – p/e

One of the most useful statistics is how much a company or market's valuation compares to the profit it makes. If a company's value (market capitalisation) is 10 times its profit then it has a p/e of 10. There is also a statistic called the forward p/e, which is just the p/e worked out on a company's published estimates for the coming year. I will not go into how the p/e for a market is calculated, but instead will list the historical values for the US stock market:

	Standard & Poor	
Year	p/e	S&P 500 index
2007	17.53	1468
2006	17.4	1418
2005	17.85	1248
2004	20.7	1211
2003	22.81	1112
2002	31.89	880
2001	46.5	1148
2000	26.41	1320
1999	30.5	1469
1998	32.6	1229
1997	24.43	970
1996	19.13	741
1995	18.14	616
1994	15.01	459
1993	21.13	466
1992	22.82	436
1991	26.12	417
1990	15.47	330
1989	15.45	353
1988	11.69	277

You do not need to be a mathematician to see that it seems better to buy into a market when the p/e is lower. The average of the last 25 years has been approximately 20.

Using p/e to spot good buys in individual shares is more complex but most skilled investors will know the issues so I will not repeat them here. However, remember that each market sector (financial, utilities, petrochemicals, etc.) will have its own historical market average for p/e. Also beware that p/e can be affected by one-off charges in a company's annual accounts, so do your research carefully.

Stock market yield versus gilts

A stock market indicator that has often signalled the end of a bear market is when the yield from the UK's FTSE 100 goes higher than the yield from 10-year gilts. You can see the logic in this indica-tor, because money tends to follow

> money tends to follow good returns

good returns, so if the stock market is yielding well then more people will want to buy shares. As with all these indicators, it should be combined with other indicators and your own, and your advisers', instincts about a market.

Directors' stock purchases

Another good indicator of the end of a bear market is when the ratio of buys to sells of directors in their own companies breaks through 13. Again, you can see the logic in this indicator. If lots of directors think their company's shares are cheap enough to put their own money into them then the market as a whole may well be cheap.

Property values

There are two statistics that commonly are used to measure the housing market. The first, and more reliable in my opinion, is the ratio of average house prices to average earnings. The second is the percentage of an average person's income that goes in mortgage payments when they first take out a mortgage. The average over the years of the first statistic is about 3.5. The peak at the 2008 crash was over 6!

Bond prices

Possibly the easiest market to predict is the corporate bond market. The financial press has spotted every major peak of interest rates that I can remember, and good commentators sensibly have recommended that their readers buy bonds.

Property companies

Companies, such as British Land, own commercial property, which they then rent out. Often the value of their properties, less their borrowings, are worth more than the sum of all their shares (their market capitalisation). If this discount to net asset value is high, and it can at times be as high as 40%, this can indicate that their shares are good value.

Bubbles, booms, crashes, bears and bulls

There is a tendency to underestimate how long all these phenomena last. The average bear market lasts 740 days and the longest one was 2,738 days. Looking at the housing market in the run up to the 2008 crash, the ratio of average house prices to average earnings was well over five for two years before the crash. The dot com bubble went on for at least six months longer than I expected, with companies earning no profits having phantasmagoric valuations. Time and again these trends last so long that many commentators start to believe that the basic laws of economics have been abolished.

brilliant tip

If it looks like a bubble it probably is. So-called contrarian investors put their money in investments that are out of fashion, rather than the latest fashion. Most successful fund managers would describe themselves to a greater or lesser extent as contrarian investors.

brilliant example

When I started writing this book oil was selling at $150 a barrel and the papers were full of tips that the commodity market was the place to make big profits. Today, as I type this chapter, oil is at $97 a barrel and is still falling fast.

Takeovers

Although investors in individual stocks and shares probably will know what they are doing, I will conclude this section with two useful pointers. The first such pointer is that nearly all mega mergers and takeovers do not work out well. I would seriously consider selling shares in a company embarking on this risky course of action.

Things usually go from bad to worse

If a company issues a profit warning, it will usually be the first of a number of such warnings. Active investors may want to consider bailing out after the first profit warning.

brilliant definition

Companies can ask their shareholders for extra investment by offering them additional shares at a discount – called a rights issue. This is a bit of a con but, unless the share price falls below the offer price, it is my experience that it is usually best to bite the bullet and buy the rights issue.

So what should you do about investments?

I have given lots of information and many tips, but I thought I ought to get off the fence and say what I am trying to do with my own investments.

First off, I hope you will have got your savings ready for your retirement well before you retire. I did not, and it will take me many years to sort them out without losing quite a lot of value or taking big risks.

Decide how much cash you need in instant-access savings accounts to cover emergencies. Personally I aim to keep more than £10,000 in instant access.

Then decide on how much you will keep in cash, but in higher interest accounts or bank and building society bonds, or savings certificates from NS&I. This will provide a safe buffer that will help you sleep well at night and that you can be sure will always be available to sell in order to cover any major expenses. Remember not to keep too much with any one institution – we now know banks and building societies are not totally safe from failing. Personally I aim to keep at least 20% of my savings in cash because I am quite risk averse.

Decide how much of the rest of your savings you want in corporate bonds. Ideally these should be in an ISA wrapper so the income is tax-free. The amount of bonds you invest in will depend on how risk averse you are, and how sure you want to be that you can maintain a good investment income even when interest rates are low. It is essential that you buy bonds when interest rates are high. The maximum I would advise putting into corporate bonds would be 20% of your savings.

I intend to put the rest of my savings into the stock market. If you are not a knowledgeable stock market investor I would recommend the bulk of your equities be in a wide range of high-income investment trusts. In my opinion these offer the best chance of getting a decent income and protecting your capital from inflation over the long term. They also have the added benefit that if you do not need all the income then reinvesting the income makes them one of the best high-growth investments available to you. Given I have warned against putting all your eggs in one basket, is this risky advice? I think the risk is acceptable for the following reasons:

● These are collective investments so really you are investing in many different shares.

● Investment trusts have a very good track record of combining both income and growth (although 2008 was a horrible year for them).

- High-income investment trusts will own shares in most market sectors, probably the main areas that will be missing are mining and technology stocks.

- Most market sectors have a number of companies paying high dividends so your investments will be spread over a large number of companies, so any one going bust is not going to hurt you too badly.

- If you are a UK investor then the bulk of your shares will be invested in the UK, but in an increasingly globalised world this is not a huge risk.

- There will be a majority of your investment in larger, safer (blue chip) companies, but there will be the diversity of some smaller companies.

- Companies that pay high dividends tend fiscally to be quite conservative.

Additional equity investments to consider are:

- small companies investment trusts
- shares in a commercial property company or investment trust.

You should build your portfolio using pound cost averaging, or using the knowledge I have given about how to buy at opportune times.

brilliant tip

Spread your savings amongst many high-income investment trusts. There is plenty of evidence that picking such trusts at random is as successful as using their past performance to guide you. There is even a monkey called Leonard on US TV who on average does as well (or as badly) as an investment expert!

So what should you do about pensions?

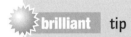 **tip**

If you have a pension fund of which you have to use a substantial part to purchase an annuity that will then provide a guaranteed annual income for the rest of your life, then check if you can shop around for the best deal. If you can shop around, usually you will be able to do much better than by sticking to your default provider who managed your pension fund. Any reputable IFA will provide you with the best deals on offer, or you can look on the internet. If you have significant health problems or are a smoker you should declare these as usually they will lead to you obtaining a better annuity. Also, think very carefully about the type of annuity you buy: it is often better to accept a significantly lower annual payment that is index linked to the annual rate of inflation; and if you have a partner they will be much safer in the long term if you accept a lower annual payment so your partner still gets all or part of your pension if you die first. Also check if you can take out a lump sum at retirement, because unless you can convert that into a pension on very favourable rates, usually you will do better to take the maximum lump sum possible.

If you are reading this book in your forties or fifties, then you need to be thinking very hard about your financial preparations for retirement. You have probably noticed that the years seem to spin round faster as you get older, and so you will not be surprised to hear me say that retirement is closer than you would like to think. You also will not be surprised by the fact that retirement probably will last much longer for you than it did for your parents – latest research suggests that around 50% of 50 year-olds will live until they are at least 90! So you'll need to have made preparations for a lengthy retirement, or be prepared to work for longer.

The government and many employers provide incentives to invest in a pension. Contributions into pension arrangements (up to prescribed limits) attract tax relief and some of the investment returns and income are also free of tax. Many employers provide contributions to your pension savings. The best employer pensions are called 'defined benefit' and pay out a lump sum and annual income based on your earnings record and the length of your service with the company. Other employer pensions are called 'defined contribution' where your contributions build up a pension pot that will pay a lump sum and also will allow you to buy an annuity to give you an income for the rest of your life. In addition there are a range of personal pension plans for people who do not have a pension from their employer.

A common question I get asked, is 'How big a pension pot, plus savings, do I need?' Provided you accept that there can be no 'one size fits all' answer to this question, I will try and give you a ballpark figure. My rough calculation is based on an estimate that, in 2008, £100,000 will purchase a joint life, index-linked annuity of approximately £4,500 p.a. for a 65-year-old male – and this is also the sort of income you could generate from a £100,000 portfolio of equities. My feeling is that if you are a higher-rate taxpayer, you are unlikely to be able to live comfortably on a pension pot, plus savings, of much less than £500,000, and if you earn much more than a basic-rate taxpayer you will need correspondingly more – frightening isn't it! How do you amass such a fortune?

brilliant tips

Do not rely on what I am saying. Pay for expert, independent financial advice as well. Also read up about the subject, so you can make informed judgements. After reading this book and seeking advice make your own mind up.

Ask for an estimate of your, and any partner's, state pension – which can be obtained from The Pension Service website. This will provide the baseline you can work from.

If you have access to a decent occupational pension scheme, where your employer makes relatively generous employer contributions, then usually it will be a no-brainer to join because your pension fund has the double advantage of tax breaks and the equivalent of extra salary. As you reach your mid forties you should be thinking about how you can make additional contributions to an additional voluntary contributions (AVC) section of your occupational pension fund. Make sure you keep an eye on the likely projections of your retirement benefits from such a scheme. I mentioned earlier in this chapter that many people do not feel confident about dealing with their finances – and if there is one area where lots of people feel least confident, it is pensions. No matter how boring or frightening you find the subject you really must not stick your head in the sand where your pension is concerned.

Sometimes you will have no control over the way your pension fund is managed. However, some pension providers give you a choice over which fund managers will invest your money, and also may allow you to choose the nature of the investment strategy that will be used. You might even have the ability to choose your pension provider.

brilliant fact

A typical default pension investment option might be as follows: 65% of your funds in equities (UK and overseas shares), and 35% in less volatile investments. A mixture of actively managed funds and passive stock market trackers will be included in the equities. Some time before retirement, usually 6–10 years, your funds will start to be moved out of the stock market and into fixed interest investments (such as government and corporate bonds) and cash investments. This ensures that your final pension pot is exposed to much lower risk of sudden drops in the stock market as you approach the time when you will be buying an annuity and taking a tax-free lump sum. As you can see it is essential that you notify your pension provider if there is a high probability that you will retire early, so that they can move your fund out of the stock market in good time.

The typical default pension option is a balance between risk and return. You may think that the default option is too conservative, and you might want higher exposure to shares, and to take personal control over when, and how fast, you move out of the stock market as you approach retirement. If you are willing to invest the time, and risk, in taking greater personal control, then you may well want to look at exploiting any options that are available to you of selecting the pension provider, fund managers and investment strategy. Most people simply do not feel comfortable making such choices and around 80% choose the default option that is offered to them.

I would advise you strongly to get free of borrowing as soon as possible – this is a very tax-efficient use of savings. In short, pay off your mortgage as quickly as possible. Apart from paying off your mortgage, what should you do about pensions and savings if you do not have access to a good occupational pension scheme? I would caution strongly against the 'property is better than pensions' mindset – read the figures I gave earlier in this chapter!

In the UK you can join a stakeholder pension, or take out a personal pension (PP), or you can do it yourself in a self-invested pension plan (SIPP). I suggest you research the pros and cons of all these options, and seek independent advice from an adviser who will not take commissions from anything you decide to do. The UK also allows you, in some circumstances (for example by having a SIPP and transferring your other pensions into it), to drawdown from your pension pot without having to buy an annuity. This is a bit riskier, but gives you and any partner of yours some significant advantages. Drawdown makes pension funds a bit more like real money, but ultimately the price you pay for the tax advantages of pensions is that pension funds are regulated so that you cannot treat them just as your own wealth. As a consequence, I would recommend that you save for your retirement by splitting your money between investments and pension contributions.

 **brilliant** definition

Income drawdown is an alternative to buying an annuity. You draw income from the investments in your pension fund by taking out interest, dividends and/or capital. The amount you can withdraw annually is limited by the Government Actuary's Department, which uses a formula that limits income to a little above the non-index linked, single life annuity that your pension pot could buy. The risks of income drawdown are obviously different to purchasing an annuity, but the big difference is that after your death your spouse or your estate will get access to your pension fund. For example, your spouse could continue income drawdown, or he/she could pay 35% tax and then get your pension savings as real money.

Warning – pension law is complex and changing all the time, so you need to check the details of income drawdown that are current when you are reading this book.

 **brilliant   tip**

Make monthly contributions to both pensions and savings.
Parkinson's Law states that your expenditure usually grows to the
size of your income, so it is best that you take the savings out each
month so that you do not think of that as money that is available
to spend. Keep increasing your monthly savings and pension
contributions as you get older and (hopefully) better paid, so that
you will have a decent-sized pension and savings to live comfortably
in your retirement. You need to review regularly the projections of
your retirement pot. You will also need to decide if you want to plan
to be in a position where you have the financial resources to take
early retirement if you want to.

If you receive lump sums, for example bonuses, inheritances or
redundancy payments, then think carefully about how to invest
them. A lot of people I talked to felt they had squandered lump
sums. If you still have a mortgage you will seldom do better than
using a lump sum to pay off part of your mortgage. Another good
option if you are a higher-rate taxpayer can be to put all or part of
a taxable lump sum into a self-invested pension plan to reduce the
amount of higher-rate tax that you have to pay.

Please learn from my mistake and ensure your savings are well
organised for when you retire.

- As you approach retirement you may decide to put most of
  your stock market investments into high-income investment
  trusts, with income reinvested. Indeed this may be your
  favoured approach for the bulk of your savings throughout
  your working life.

- Watch the market conditions so that you can buy some
  long-term corporate bonds at a propitious time in the run
  up to your retirement.

- If you have control over your pension fund then, if you see a bear market setting in as you approach retirement, you probably will want to get substantially out of the stock market so that you can buy the best possible annuity – this is much less important if you will be using income drawdown rather than purchasing an annuity.

 **tip**

As your retirement approaches it is well worth doing a budget of your outgoings, and rehearsing living on your retirement income.

CHAPTER 4

Your state
of mind

This book contains two sorts of information: firstly, there are hard facts, analysis and advice about practical subjects (money, health, maintaining your independence, etc.); secondly there are more psychological issues, such as your state of mind and relationships, and these are often the hardest ones to handle.

The $64,000 question is 'Can I control my state of mind?' The simple answer is, 'Yes you can – within limits'. This is exactly what professional counsellors and psychiatrists help their patients to do. As an example, therapy has at least as successful a track record in treating depression as modern anti-depressants do – indeed most severe cases are treated using both medication and therapy. We are all familiar with, and probably believe that 'mind over matter' works on issues such as health – and our belief is well backed up by medical statistics. But we are less aware that we can exercise mindful control over our fears, anxieties, obsessions, bad habits, intolerant attitudes, etc.

Joie de vivre

Joie de vivre not only makes you live longer, it also makes you live better. The clarion call of those with joie de vivre is, 'How did I ever find the time to go to work?' A lust for life is related to other states of mind, such as optimism, which we will come onto in more detail later, but it is a more all-encompassing attitude.

 **tips**

Do not act your age, because you will age much more slowly if you think and act like someone half your age.

When an exciting opportunity to do something turns up, stop yourself thinking of all the reasons not to do it, and think of how to solve the problems so you can say 'yes please'.

pack as much fun and fulfilment into your retired years as you can

You are a long time dead, so make the effort to pack as much fun and fulfilment into your retired years as you can.

Use it or lose it

Mental exercise has been proven to improve and then preserve your mental faculties. There are many enjoyable ways of doing this. Just a few examples are:

- bridge or other card games
- crosswords
- sudoku
- learning – such as the University of the Third Age, locally run courses, etc.
- home computing
- community or church work.

Be positive

 **tip**

My brother has helped me greatly with the research for this book.
His number one tip for a brilliant retirement is 'rule your problems,
do not let them rule you'.

I have met lots of retired people who have had to contend with
some pretty serious problems. Some had chronic health problems; others were very short of money; some had problems
because they did not, or could no longer, drive. Many of these
people refused to let these problems ruin their lives and, by
being positive, managed to make light of their problems. Often
they led much more active and happy lives than others who let
minor problems dominate their lives.

 **tip**

Stop grumbling! One of the best ways to become more positive is
to force yourself to stop voicing your negativity. It will also have the
excellent side effect of making you less irritating to your loved ones,
friends and acquaintances.

Many of the techniques I suggest are of the sort 'monkey do,
monkey feel'. You may be aware of the fact that, if you are
unhappy, then lifting your head, putting your shoulders back
and smiling has been proven to help you lift your mood.

Another useful technique to help create a positive mindset is to
'count your blessings'. I was talking to a disabled person and
asked how she managed to stay so cheerful. She told me that

she was very lucky to have enough money to pay people to help her, and that she had a son and many close friends who lived locally who provided a lot of support. My late aunt and uncle did not drive but always said how lucky they were to have found a likeable and highly reliable taxi driver. If you are not naturally positive it is well worth consciously reminding yourself about all the good things in your life.

Be optimistic

There really are two sorts of people in the world, the 'glass half full' people and the 'glass half empty' people. The link between optimism and other psychological aspects such as joie de vivre was beautifully summed up by a piece of graffiti I once read:

The world belongs to optimists – pessimists are merely spectators

Train yourself to say optimistic things, and you may be surprised that over time you will start to become more optimistic.

Another useful technique is to notice how often your pessimism is unjustified. As a personal example, I used to be very pessimistic whenever severe weather was forecast. Then I decided to note down how often the bad weather actually materialised; it was less than 50 per cent of the time! So I started to be more optimistic and even decided to stop checking the weather forecast so frequently so as to desensitise myself. I also reminded myself that now I am retired I no longer have to travel to meetings so the weather no longer has much influence on my life.

Control your fear and anxiety

A number of people I talked to said that they were so grateful that they no longer had to cope with the extreme pressures that work put them under. However, many of these same

example

After my father retired he started to hate Christmas because the country seemed to close down for over a week and he worried about what would happen if something broke (e.g. the central heating failed), or he or my mother were taken ill. Then, as he got older and became more dependent on my brother, he started to fear the times my brother went on holiday.

people said that stress expands to fill the void. In particular they allowed their fears and anxieties to fill the gap.

One problem many retired people face is that they have more time to read the daily papers and watch the news unfolding on television and the internet. This can expose you

> the doom and gloom merchants usually have been wrong in the past

to many panics and scare stories. Just remember that the doom and gloom merchants usually have been wrong in the past.

There are a number of things that you can do to control your personal fears. Firstly, you need to remember that, when things have gone wrong in the past, you have always coped, so you will cope if bad things do happen – it will not be the end of the world! Secondly, there are plenty of practical things you can do to reduce your anxiety, such as organise breakdown cover for your car/gas/central heating and other home emergencies. If you are very worried about power cuts then buy a portable generator. Other people pay for private medical insurance for the feeling of security it gives them. Another good technique is to ask yourself, 'What is the worst that can happen?' You usually will find that there will be some way you can cope. The final technique is to think about whether worrying about something does any good – usually it does not.

What about the biggies – aging, death, disability, etc?

Acceptance

There is a wise saying that you should 'change what you can, and accept what you cannot change'. People with strong religious beliefs are at a great advantage in accepting life's tribulations. However, you do not need to believe in a higher authority to accept the things you cannot change. Remind yourself that acceptance is the best way to cope with the things you cannot change – if you cannot accept the inevitable you will only make yourself miserable. Taking the extreme example of facing your own death, I would add the optimistic observation that the majority of people face death with courage and dignity, and nowadays the NHS and charities are well set up to help you do this.

> change what you can, and accept what you cannot change

Another area where acceptance is very important is in your relationships with loved ones, friends and acquaintances. You are unlikely to be able to change people's personalities. You may be able to stop a relationship breaking down by drawing the other person's attention to some aspect of their behaviour. However, in many cases you will be happiest if you accept people just for who they are – warts and all. This is partly acceptance and partly tolerance.

Tolerance

In my opinion one of the less pleasant aspects of aging is that retired people sometimes become less and less tolerant as they get older. It is not at all uncommon to meet elderly people whose politics have moved far to the right of Attila the Hun. Such people often will become overtly racist and also rage against 'scroungers', 'immigrants', 'bureaucrats', 'the youth of today', 'the government', 'the European Union (or other political organisation)' – I am sure you can complete the list yourself.

 **tip**

Who am I to tell you what your politics should be? I am not suggesting you suddenly become more liberal, but I will make a thoroughly practical point. People who become increasingly intolerant and angry about society, who go on, and on, and on, ad nauseum about their intolerant attitudes, are very *boring*. In particular, many younger people will find such views extremely offensive. My advice is, if you feel this way, then shut up unless you know your listeners are all like-minded.

If you constantly say 'when I was young we …' then it is much less likely that you will mix with young people, which brings me on to the next point.

Stay in touch with the real world

It is so easy to lose touch with the real world. I have noticed that, even after just 18 months of retirement, I am already forgetting what it was like to go to work every day. When I meet my ex-colleagues I am surprised by how strange their lives seem. I have partly forgotten the pressures and stresses that most working people have to survive – meetings arranged and rearranged at short notice, unreasonable customers, incompetent managers, reorganisations, office politics – I can hardly bear to type this list.

I also remember my brother and sister complaining how my parents had forgotten about the reality of bringing up children, and that they did not understand that modern parents faced many pressures that the older generation had been spared. Another problem is that every generation feels that the younger generation has it much easier than they did, forgetting that there are flipsides, such as the increased pace of work and home life, the fact that occupational pensions are generally much less generous, etc.

There is a slightly naughty saying that a man is 'only as old as the woman he feels'. I would like to rephrase this as the cleaner and more useful saying, 'You are only as old as the people you associate with'. When talking to young people, do use your ears as well as your mouth, and try not to lecture or bore them – and remember my advice about not being a vocal, grumpy, old fascist.

you are only as old as the people you associate with

I suggest that you take an interest in current affairs. Also, try to stay up to date with modern cultural phenomena and technology. Get computer literate and send emails and photos to loved ones and friends, join a social networking website, text your children/nieces/nephews, watch the latest hit TV show, etc. At our swimming pool we have a computer-literate 92-year-old, so age does not disbar you from accessing modern technology.

brilliant tip

You will find that many of the younger generation will help you with modern technology if you express an interest; not only will this help you to get to grips with the technology faster than any textbook, it is an opportunity to build relationships with younger people.

In my research many retired people mentioned that travel was an excellent way of helping them stay in touch and they recommended travel as an excellent source of social and mental stimulation.

tip

Do not live in the past. Do not dwell on past mistakes or bad luck. Do not bear long-term grudges.

Maintain your flexibility

In Chapter 3 we looked at adjusting to retired life and developing a new routine. While this is important, many of the people I talked to highlighted the danger of letting your routine become too rigid. So, if you find yourself passing up opportunities to do something different because it conflicts with your routine, it is probably time to remember that your routine is your servant, not your master.

> your routine is your servant, not your master

The darkest sides of routines are obsessions and rituals. You need to watch for these developing and help your friends and loved ones avoid them, and ask them to warn you if you are developing such unhealthy symptoms.

brilliant **tip**

Because all the psychological issues I am discussing are inter-related, you will be pleasantly surprised how progress in one area will often spill over into other areas.

Be sociable

As already mentioned, your social network is a valuable commodity, one that should stretch well outside your immediate family. Research shows that the size and strength of your social network is a key factor in your health, happiness and independence. It is also the perfect defence against that most frightening aspect of aging – loneliness.

There are some very obvious things you should avoid if you want a wide and supportive social network. I hope some will be extremely obvious; ignore them and you will find your network shrinking rapidly – so do not be:

- rude
- aggressive
- moaning
- angry
- grumpy
- intolerant
- boring
- inconsiderate
- self-centred
- boastful
- a show-off
- demanding
- someone that does not say please and thank you.

I am sure you can add to this list! There are, however, some subtler issues that are well worth mentioning.

I can divide my friends into two sorts: those that I am sure would help if I was in trouble, and the others. If you are someone who is willing to help people in need, then you will have a much wider circle of friends.

Another important skill to learn is the ability to really listen – it is something we can all work on. Good listeners develop the knack of putting themselves in other people's positions. Good listeners are often those who offer sound advice and comments. If you are a good listener not only are you more likely to have a wider group of friends, but people tend to forgive you a lot, for example a boring person who is a good listener will probably have lots of friends.

You need to accept that relationships require effort. So:

- be willing to initiate contacts with strangers
- maintain contacts with your existing friends
- make an effort to offer and return hospitality
- be generous and thoughtful.

Independent minded

Many people I talked to, especially those who had lost their partner, strongly advised me to recommend that you develop your independence of mind.

develop your independence of mind

To be independent minded you need to be willing to do things on your own, so that you do not have just shared interests, shared activities and shared friends. You will also want to make your own decisions, or at the very least contribute to shared decisions. Finally, do not be afraid to have your own opinions, and be willing to voice them and defend them.

 **example**

A widow I talked to said that the fact that she worked in a charity shop was a real lifesaver when her husband died because she had a circle of friends in the shop to talk to.

If you rely on someone else for important aspects of your life, then you need to have at least a basic understanding of how to do them yourself, or how you can find someone else to do them for you. For example, if your partner handles all the financial issues get them to explain to you how to do all the basic things, and show you where all the information is kept; or you may get your partner to show one of your children where everything is. As another example, if your partner does all the cooking, get them to show you how to cook simple meals.

 **tip**

If you are suffering from bereavement there are many very helpful resources you can read. Typing 'coping with bereavement' into an internet search engine will find numerous sites with excellent guidance and leaflets.

A final word

Ask your partner, close family and best friends to help you monitor and improve your state of mind. In extreme cases you may need to talk to a therapist or counsellor, but in the major-ity of cases those closest to you will help you keep a positive, healthy mindset.

CHAPTER 5

Managing
your health

Current research into aging is producing very optimistic results. Most people who retire can look forward to a long period in which health issues can be managed effectively so that they do not impact your quality of life significantly. This chapter will give you many tips on how to maximise both the length and quality of what can be the best period of your life.

There is a humorous saying that, 'If I had known I was going to live this long then I would have looked after myself better.' The good news is that few of your habits will have done significant lasting damage and changing your habits now will improve greatly your longevity and your quality of life. A retired person has much more space in their life to make these changes than they had when they were on the career treadmill.

In this chapter we will look at the top three areas in which you can make a substantial difference to your quality and quantity of life – diet, exercise and, if appropriate, giving up smoking. Little of what I will say is anything more than common sense, but you know what they say about common sense – it is a very uncommon sense.

Eating habits

There really is no secret to healthy eating – eat a balanced diet. Try not to eat any type of food too frequently, and eat a bit of everything. Research indicates the following list of do's and don'ts.

- Do eat wholegrain in preference to white bread.
- Do include fish, especially oily fish, regularly within your diet.
- Do eat freshly prepared food frequently, and don't eat too many ready meals and take-aways – not to mention that freshly prepared food is likely to be tastier and cheaper (retired people have more time to cook than the worker bees).
- Do eat at least five portions of fresh fruit or vegetables a day – if you have a garden you could even try growing them yourself.
- Don't drink too much alcohol (less than 3 to 4 units of alcohol a day for men, and 2 to 3 units for women, where a unit is about half a pint of 4% ABV beer). And no, you cannot save them up for a binge!
- Don't eat large amounts of red meat.
- Don't eat too much processed food.
- Don't eat excessive amounts of sugar. So you need to be sensible about the amount of confectionery you eat (yes, that does include chocolate!).
- Don't overdo the amount of salt you eat.
- Don't eat excessive amounts of saturated fat (sorry, that does include cheese).

If you have food intolerances or are a vegetarian then you should ask your doctor for advice on how best to maintain a balanced diet.

There is very little advice that applies specifically to older people. You should avoid fizzy drinks to lessen the risk of osteoporosis, which affects men as well as women. You should also be careful to avoid being overweight or eating too much refined sugar, to reduce the chances of developing late-onset diabetes. Other than that you should just stick to a balanced diet.

One of the advantages of eating a balanced diet is that you will be able to safely ignore most food-scare stories in the press.

Most of us at some point will wish we could lose a few pounds in weight, and some of us may even feel we need to lose a lot of weight. The medical benefits of keeping your weight under control are well proven. The most common measure used to determine if you are over- or underweight is the body mass index (BMI). You can calculate your BMI by measuring your weight in kilograms and dividing it by the square of your height in metres. Typically, if your BMI is in the range of 18.5 to 25 then you would not be considered as overweight or underweight. So, if you are overweight, you need to go on a diet – *wrong* – in my view this is not the best way to approach losing weight.

What you eat regularly has a certain number of calories, with a particular mix of protein, fat and carbohydrates and, together with the amount of exercise you take, has led to you stabilising at your current weight. If you change your eating and exercise habits permanently then you will stabilise at a different weight. The word diet-

> losing weight is easy, it is keeping it off that is hard

ing suggests a phase when you lose weight, but losing weight is easy, it is keeping it off that is hard.

The best thing to do is to focus on what your long-term eating habits are going to be. Indeed, there is evidence that extreme diets, either with very few calories or those that unbalance a diet (e.g. low carbohydrate), will lead to a situation where your steady-state weight for a particular long-term diet actually will increase. I recommend strongly that you avoid all extreme diets.

The good news is that short periods where you eat more, such as holidays and Christmas, will have only a temporary effect and, when you return to your normal eating habits, then your weight will return to the normal level.

Unsurprisingly, the key to your new eating habits, leading to a new, thinner body, is to reduce your calorie intake – permanently. By eating many different foodstuffs in moderation, you will not go far wrong.

There is a very substantial industry that has grown up around dieting. There are well-regarded clubs that recommend eating a balanced diet, which can provide valuable moral support. There are also some diet plans such as the fashionable GI diet that promote healthy eating habits.

 **tip**

You do not have to make a single large jump to your new eating regime. In fact there is a lot to be said for doing it in a few steps. Try not to be in a hurry.

Although there are some parts of the slimming industry that are best avoided, the industry has also produced lots of common-sense advice and good products to help you reduce calories and maintain a balanced diet, with the minimum impact on your lifestyle.

Smaller portions have fewer calories

Probably the simplest way to cut down on calories is to eat smaller portions. Half a cream cake has half the calories of the whole cake (surprise!). Speaking of cream cakes ...

Cut down on food you know is fattening

You know that cakes, sticky puddings, lashings of cream, chocolate and deep-fried anything are very fattening. If you eat lots of them, then you are unlikely to stabilise at a weight you are happy with.

Cut down on frying with fat/oil

Food fried with oil or fat is always full of calories. If you love chips then there are many good-tasting oven chips that have many fewer calories than deep-fried 'proper' chips. There are also excellent non-stick frying pans that allow you to dry fry or fry with just a little (unsaturated fat) oil.

Take-aways should be treats not a regular part of your diet

Most take-aways are very fattening, as well as often being full of salt.

 **tip**

Do not cut naughty things out of your diet totally, just reduce them so that they become treats.

Use diet soft drinks

If you cannot kick the fizzy drink habit altogether it is worth the effort to change over to sugar-free alternatives.

Eat low-calorie nibbles

Many of us are nibblers, so swap from the crisps and chocolate bars to fruit, vegetables and low-calorie snacks.

Fresh cooked food should rule, OK!

Fresh cooked food with fresh ingredients potentially has a lot fewer calories than ready prepared meals and processed foods.

Alcohol

Once you no longer have the stresses of work it is much easier to reduce your alcohol consumption. Following the government's advice on the maximum number of alcohol units that should be consumed a week obviously is best. Statistically there is a one in three chance that you the reader regularly drink more than the advised limits. From my own experience I found that reducing my consumption (by about a third) helped me lose weight, sleep better, have fewer headaches and, given that I really like the feeling of mild intoxication, I found that within a month I was getting the same buzz from the reduced consumption. It also helps the finances!

As you can see, nothing about improving your eating habits is rocket science. The potential benefits from an increased, good-quality lifespan, and a better self-image are very significant indeed.

Exercise

The benefits of regular exercise are well proven in terms of reduced mortality and morbidity. I probably do not have to convince you that you will look better, feel better and be able to do more without getting tired. In addition you may well find that you sleep better.

The key to a successful exercise regime is to build it in as a natural and regular part of your routine. Without the demands of work, retired people tend to find it much easier to take regular exercise than the worker bees. There is no best form of exercise, but here are three ideas for starters:

● Walking
　– It is very easy to build walking into your daily life.
　– There are no special skills or equipment required.

- It is very cheap.
- It can be pursued as a solitary or a social activity.
- Aerobic exercise (where your heart rate speeds up) can be achieved easily by not taking lifts and escalators.
- It is very safe.
- It does not develop the muscles in the upper body.
- It is excellent for building stamina.
- It can help prevent problems such as osteoporosis.

- Swimming
  - Probably the safest form of exercise that develops muscles in the whole body, because the water takes the strain off your skeleton.
  - It is very good for people with bad backs.
  - Ear infections can be a problem.
  - A nearby pool may not be available.
  - In the UK it is now free for the over sixties.
  - Also it can be either a social or a solitary activity.

- Join a gym
  - Working out can develop the whole body, and can achieve the most marked improvement in your physical appearance.
  - Some people find it boring, although group activities such as aerobics can be more stimulating.
  - Minor injuries are quite common.
  - Membership varies from moderate to very expensive.
  - They tend to be available widely in towns.
  - It can be a social or a solitary activity.

In addition, hobbies such as gardening, dancing and golf can provide plenty of exercise, although gardening tends to be a seasonal activity.

 **brilliant** tips

If you start to take more exercise then build up your exercise routine gradually. Many health professionals give the sound advice that you should 'listen to your body'. When exercising this is a very sensible approach.

Exercise can be a useful way of making friends. In addition, if exercise becomes a social activity you are much more likely to keep doing it regularly. Going to a gym or swimming pool at the same time each day makes it much likelier you will get to know other people.

Give up smoking

When writing this book in general, and this chapter in particular, I did not want to preach at you, but I am about to do exactly that. If you are a smoker then my medical adviser, Dr Margaret Grant, says I should tell you in the strongest possible terms to stop. Statistics about the dangers of smoking are simply dreadful. I used to smoke, and I adored smoking, but in the end I just could not ignore the terrible dangers involved. Not only is smoking quite likely to kill or damage you, the ways it does so are not

brilliant fact

A non-smoker who retires at 50 is twice as likely to see their 60th birthday than someone who smokes 20 a day. If the thought of a premature, unpleasant death does not worry you, how about going blind? The most common cause of blindness in the over sixties is age-related macular degeneration (AMD). A smoker is three times as likely to develop AMD as a non-smoker.

nice at all. For example, smoking is implicated strongly in cancers of the lung, oesophagus, tongue, throat and tonsils.

If you give up smoking, some residual risk from past smoking remains, but your life expectancy and chance of encountering other smoking-related health problems declines very quickly. After you have retired is an excellent time to quit. You no longer need the nicotine to help cope with the pressures of work, and withdrawal symptoms will not affect your performance at work. In addition your income probably has just gone down so the money saved is likely to be very welcome.

Apart from saving money there are numerous other benefits in giving up. Your sense of taste will get much better. You will no longer be setting a bad example to grandchildren and/or nieces and nephews. You will not subject others to the not inconsiderable dangers of passive smoking. Some benefits, such as increased fertility, probably do not interest you personally but, by helping set a good example to the younger generations, you may have a better chance of having a lot more youngsters to spoil.

brilliant tip

Apart from withdrawal symptoms, the main downside to giving up smoking is that you probably will put on weight. For this reason it can be a good idea to combine quitting smoking with the move to a healthier, lower calorie diet.

In those countries where smoking is banned in restaurants, pubs and bars it is certainly easier to quit smoking than it used to be. The urge to light up after a meal or with a drink used to cause many a lapse, and those situations are now much less common. Indeed the whole social aspect of smoking has virtually disappeared in many countries.

There is clear evidence that seeking help from your doctor greatly increases the chances of quitting successfully. The use of nicotine patches or gum can be very effective indeed.

 **tip**

Why not put the book down and make an appointment to see your doctor now – and if you do, I may have just saved you from a long and lingering death (how many authors can say that!).

Giving up smoking is the most obvious positive action you can take to live longer. Diet and exercise have already been mentioned, but what other things should you do to promote a long and happy life?

 **fact**

A study in 2009, led by the Centers for Disease Control and Prevention in Atlanta, USA, measured the benefit of combining weight control, not smoking, eating a healthy diet and taking regular exercise. Their figures show a 93 per cent reduction in diabetes, 81 per cent reduction in heart attacks, 50 per cent reduction in strokes and a reduction in cancer of 36 per cent.

Proactive health management

Before discussing what to do it is worth saying what you should not do – do not become obsessed with your health. Your purpose in living longer should be to have more enjoyment, fulfilment, friendship and love. People who are obsessed with their health usually do not have much fun and are not much fun to be around. However, there is quite a lot you can do apart from eating healthily, controlling your weight, exercising and not smoking.

Most doctors' surgeries in most countries will run 'well person' clinics, which will give you regular blood tests, blood pressure checks and general lifestyle advice. It is a very good idea to attend such clinics, particularly because they will ensure you get regular cholesterol and blood pressure checks. This is important because high cholesterol and high blood pressure increase the risk of heart disease and strokes significantly, and given that there are now effective drug treatments that can easily solve these problems it is well worth the effort.

You should attend all regular screenings – for example, women should attend their regular mammogram and cervical smear appointments. Some tests are not yet part of screening programmes but you can ask for them. For example, there is now an excellent screening test for bowel cancer, and catching it early dramatically improves survival rates. My medical adviser says she thinks men should ask for a prostate-specific antigen test (PSA test) to screen for possible prostate cancer. The PSA test produces a numeric result, which you will need to discuss with your doctor to determine what, if any, further tests are necessary. You should also do self-screening: women should check their breasts regularly and men should check their testes.

Many conditions, such as diabetes, high cholesterol, high blood pressure and glaucoma, can be inherited from your parents and grandparents. If you know you are susceptible to any inherited conditions obviously it makes sense to act appropriately to minimise the risk to yourself.

brilliant tip

Do not worry about having to take drugs to control cholesterol, blood pressure (or other dangerous conditions) for the rest of your life. They are a major factor in increased longevity.

On the other hand do be careful not to become dependent on over-the-counter medication, such as painkillers. Taken too regularly such medication can have unpleasant or dangerous side effects.

 **tip**

When receiving medical treatment or drugs – do as you are instructed. Many people do themselves harm by not following directions.

See your dentist and your optician regularly

See your dentist and your optician regularly. A good optician can detect:

- the early onset of glaucoma (high pressure in the eye, which is highly treatable but will blind you if left untreated)
- age-related macular degeneration (which is not yet curable, but can be managed partially if detected early)
- diabetes (which if not treated can blind you)
- high blood pressure.

A good dentist not only looks after your teeth and gums, but will also look for other abnormalities, such as cancer of the tongue.

You need to be aware of your body and see your doctor if you think you may need tests or treatment. Some of the symptoms that should not be ignored include:

- chest pains
- shortness of breath
- persistent cough
- unexplained weight loss
- dizziness
- changes in your bowel habits

- unexplained feelings of extreme tiredness
- new skin lesions that do not heal
- impotence
- blood in your excretions.

 **brilliant** tip

Try not to be obsessed about cancer. Most symptoms will not turn out to be cancer, so do not put off going to the doctor. Even if it is cancer, the survival rates for many cancers are now excellent, especially if detected early. Treatments for cancer are improving all the time.

It is worth saying when you should not visit your doctor. If you have the flu or one of the bugs that is doing the rounds (such as diarrhoea and vomiting) just self medicate, take painkillers and lots of fluids. Your pharmacist can be very helpful in managing the symptoms of common bugs. Only if symptoms persist because you have, say, developed a chest infection, should you visit your doctor.

NHS versus private health care

Many countries have a state-funded health care system (which I will refer to by the UK name of the National Health Service, or NHS for short), as well as a range of private health care providers. But when is it worth using a private health care provider?

Dr Grant believes that if you have an acute or life-threatening problem you are best to stick with the NHS. However, all national health systems have to ration care (usually through waiting lists) and, although treatment for acute and life-threatening conditions is usually excellent, you cannot be confident that the NHS is going to provide convenient and timely care for conditions that are not urgent or life threatening. As an example, if you have back, neck, leg, shoulder or foot pain, then the supply of physiotherapists, osteopaths, chiropractors and chiropodists available through the NHS is so limited you may do best to pay if you can afford it.

For other problems such as cataracts and joint replacements, you may want to be able to specify when you are treated, or want the confidence that you know precisely who will be operating on you. Some people may want to avoid the lack of privacy and perceptions about the prevalence of superbug infections in NHS hospitals. If you can afford it, you may want to either have medical insurance, or pay as you go, for such treatments. Apart from the cost, the main downsides of private medical care are that many private hospitals do not have facilities for critical care nursing and resident medical cover – which means that if something goes seriously wrong you may need to be taken by ambulance to an NHS hospital.

What about alternative therapies, such as aromatherapy, reflexology, herbalists, acupuncture, hypnotherapy and homeopathy? While these can work as a complement to your doctor's care, I would warn against using such therapies in place of conventional medical treatments. Therapies such as aromatherapy, reflexology, acupuncture and homeopathy are unlikely to have dangerous side effects and, if you can afford them and they help you, why not use them? But be careful of those therapies that have a powerful effect, but are not scientifically understood, such as herbal preparations.

In a similar vein, should you take diet supplements? Dr Grant says that if you eat a balanced diet you do not need supplements. She also warns strongly against taking large doses of any supplements. However, moderate doses will harm only your wallet and if you find them helpful there is no reason to avoid them.

Scientific facts and falsehoods

I have already alerted the reader to beware of the latest food scares, which are often based on very dubious statistics. There are, however, some statistics that are definitely worth reporting.

There is a very close correlation between the number of people you are close to and your health. The larger your social network, the healthier you are likely to be and the longer you will live. I think that this may be linked to another finding: people who say they are 'satisfied' and 'active' are likely to be healthier and live longer.

There is a well-publicised untruth, which is that the average person loses 10,000 brain neurons a day. In tests on rats it has been shown that if elderly rats are kept in the company of other rats, in surroundings with toys that give them lots of stimulation, their brains enlarge. On the other hand, the brains of elderly rats kept in isolation deteriorate. Obviously these tests cannot prove that the same thing happens in humans, but there were ethical difficulties in persuading the authorities to allow the scientists to cut live people's heads open!

My interpretation of these results suggests that happy, active people, with lots of friends and relatives, will make considerable use of their mental and physical faculties, which will have a significant benefit on their health. Or, to repeat the old adage, 'use it, or lose it'. You also seem to have the circular effect, that being healthy makes you happy and being happy makes you healthy.

> use it, or lose it

Researchers into aging frequently make the point that people are not just blessed or cursed by their genes. Certainly, some people are naturally more active, less anxious and have a more positive attitude than other people with less sunny dispositions.

Research does seem to show that people can use their free will to become more active, less anxious and more outgoing.

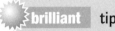 **tip**

Starting retirement can be a major shock to your system. It is likely that you will be adjusting to lower levels of adrenaline as the stress of work ceases. Do not be alarmed by the fact that temporarily you may suffer mood swings, depression, sleep problems, etc. My advice is not to be in a great hurry to make significant changes to your life immediately after you retire – wait until you feel you have established a new, stable routine in your life.

Handling common ailments

It is not possible to fully disentangle all the challenges that retired people face from the problems that you will have to manage as you get older. However, let's take a look at the most common health issues highlighted in my research.

Depression

Men in particular become much more susceptible to depression as they get older. If the depression is starting to become debilitating you should consult your doctor. Many people have been helped by the latest generation of anti-depressants.

One of the greatest protections against serious depression is to have a large social network. The best treatment for depression often is just talking about those issues that depress you. Friends and relatives may not be trained, but often will be excellent counsellors. If depression becomes debilitating then the services of a trained therapist or counsellor can often be very successful in overcoming the depression. Do not be put off by the outdated images of Freudian-style therapists or the names of the latest fashionable therapies (e.g. cognitive-based therapy (CBT) and Mindfulness). A good therapist or counsellor will apply many well-tried techniques that are designed to help you understand and manage your unhelpful thoughts, emotions, fears and anxieties.

Sleep problems

If you put the two words *sleep* and *problems* into a search engine such as Google you will get a wealth of well-researched advice from organisations such as the Royal College of Psychiatrists. All the reputable sites give very similar advice.

brilliant tip

The internet can be a source of excellent medical information and advice. However, be careful to check whether the source of the advice is trustworthy. Check numerous reputable sites to ensure that facts or advice are repeated by more than one reliable source. Beware of taking advice from newsgroups, chat rooms and the like.

The medical profession don't always give you accurate or full information. The internet is one of the best ways of checking whether you need to ask for a second opinion.

Common advice to manage sleep problems includes:

● Beware taking prescribed sleeping pills for anything other than a short period. Even the latest sleeping pills are addictive, lose their effectiveness over time and can leave you feeling dopey during the day. Many over the counter preparations suffer similar, but less severe, problems. If homeopathic remedies work for you then these are ideal because they seem to have no unpleasant side effects. If you are taking prescription sleeping pills regularly, the advice of experts is to discuss with your doctor how you can safely wean yourself off them.

- Create a good sleeping environment.
- Avoid taking naps during the day.
- Take plenty of exercise.
- Do not use alcohol to get to sleep; you will probably wake up in the night and find it harder to get back to sleep.
- Do not get obsessed about not sleeping; you are retired so do not have to go to work in the morning.

The last point can be so significant that if you are getting very uptight about sleep problems then it may be worth seeking the services of a trained counsellor/therapist.

Bones and joint problems

If you are unlucky enough to suffer from fractures or joints wearing out, then you will benefit from the fact that ortho-paedic surgery is now very well advanced. You should consult your 'well person' clinic about the best preventative measures, such as weight loss, diet and regular exercise. You can also take care when walking down stairs or in slippery conditions – but unfortunately this is one of the risks of getting old.

Likewise there are a number of nasty forms of rheumatism and arthritis that can, at best, be managed. However, at the time of writing, progress on treating such problems offers hope for the future.

have a positive attitude of mind

The best way to cope well with such problems is to have a posi-tive attitude of mind. They can ruin your life – if you let them.

 **brilliant** tips

If you have a chronic health problem then you should rule it – do not let it rule you!

Beware the potentially fatal vicious circle where you take life too easy, so you eat less or put on weight, become unfit, and feel permanently tired and hence feel even less like doing anything.

Some final advice

Do not wrap yourself in cotton wool. Although I have no research to back it up, I suspect members of extreme sports clubs have a longer than average life expectancy – and if they do not, they will have packed more experiences into their shorter lives. I was there when a member of the UK's special forces was asked what the death rate was in the SAS. He replied, 'Exactly the same as the rest of the population: one person, one death.' There is only one end to retirement, which is death, so you should concentrate on maximising the amount of quality life you have before then.

CHAPTER 6

Relationships

A big surprise for me was the number of people who high-lighted problems with relationships with their loved ones as one of the biggest issues they faced after retirement.

Your partner

This was one issue I had spotted, but the range of different sit-uations and problems took me aback. Here is some advice on how to deal with the most common issues.

Your partner is a housewife or house-husband

Provided you are both aware of the issues that can arise there need be no problems. However, if you are not aware that there may be problems you are about to embark on a journey that is about as safe as playing hopscotch in a minefield.

 **tip**

Talk to your partner about likely problems before you retire. This means that you can plan solutions in advance and, if you encounter problems, you can talk them through rather than having blinding rows, or pained silences (which can be even worse).

example

The saddest story I heard was when a man retired from a physical job he decided that he was going to have a holiday for the rest of his life. His holiday entailed his wife waiting on him – hand, foot and finger. The worst part of this story is that his wife went along with it and, to make matters worse, he died of natural causes rather than being killed by her.

Just because your partner enjoys your company on holiday, it does not mean they are not going to have their life severely disrupted by having you around the house all the time.

There are many potential problems that need to be addressed.

Your partner is used to being the boss round the home

You were the breadwinner, and your partner ran the home. It is unlikely that your partner is going to take kindly to you assuming that you will now make the decisions in your home life. On the other hand it is reasonable for you to want to have a say in how the home is run. There are no right and wrong answers here, but if you and your partner do not communicate well then do not come whining to me when you step on a landmine!

Negotiate new daily routines

To illustrate the point, consider the following question: 'What time are we normally going to get up in the morning?'

You and your partner now have the freedom to make new choices, but if you change the time you both get up then your partner will have to adapt their routine to cope with a lie-in in the mornings (strangely, I did not meet any couples who chose to get up earlier!). This is not a trivial issue because a leading UK researcher into retirement found that the freedom to have a lie-in was high up the list that the subjects of her research reported of the main benefits of retirement.

 **tips**

> I recommend that your starting point should be that your partner's routine will be as little altered as possible. You probably will find then that your partner suggests changes, and you can jointly discuss which ones you make. There is no hurry to make these changes – take things slowly and see what works.
>
> A good way to make space for positive changes in your partner's routine is to offer to do some of the chores. If you are a man reading this book, then I have some bad news for you – there really is no reason why you cannot help clean the house, put the rubbish out, etc.

Give each other space

I have a suspicion that there is often a fine dividing line between 'it is nice that we see more of each other now' and getting on each other's nerves. So it should come as no surprise that my next recommendation is that you pursue individual interests, have your own friends and have your own separate spaces in the house or garden where you can be on your own.

Your partner retires while you continue to work

When this happened to me I really wished I had known that it could be such an unsettling experience. There are a number of reasons for this, some of which I will deal with here, and others will be covered in the next section where the situation is reversed (you retire and your partner continues to work).

The main issue is that you and your partner no longer share the experience of pursuing a career and you alone face the pressures of working. You will find that your conversations at home with your partner change rapidly, as their interests will change dramatically. The solution is to make sure you both show an interest in what the other has been doing during the day, and what they plan for the days ahead.

Now listen very carefully, this is important – your partner's new purpose in life is not to make life easy for you. The wife of a couple in this position used to write her husband long lists of things to do. Even when asked to stop she continued to write them. They separated for two years! I'm sure your partner will be happy to do extra to support you, just don't expect more than they are happy to give. Remember they will have new goals and ambitions to pursue.

 **tip**

> It is difficult not to be jealous of your partner's new life. Envy is fine, but jealousy is not! Remember that they will also have twinges of envy about the faster-paced life you lead at work.

You retire while your partner continues to work

You need to remember that your partner is still facing the pressures of work, and act accordingly. Nagging your partner because they have to rush off on urgent trips and meetings at short notice, work long hours, bring work home (just like you used to) is not fair. In fact, investing part of your wonderful new life in making things easier for your partner would not be unreasonable. You will find that you will probably have much more energy than your partner, and you need to be careful about wanting to do more things than they physically can cope with – although if you have done some of their weekend chores you may find they are delighted to go out more.

 **brilliant** tip

If your partner is still enjoying work then do not put pressure on them to retire, even if you could manage financially if they did.

General relationship advice

If you have any problems in your relationship they are quite likely to deteriorate after you retire. A classic example is couples who argue about money – this will get a lot worse when you have less to live on.

Most couples sweep their problems under the carpet, but when you retire it may well be better to start talking to each other about any problems you have. Because this can be a quite painful process there is no shame at all in seeing a professional counsellor. I have received excellent feedback about the effectiveness of relationship counselling.

Do you remember to show your partner that you still love them? Do you tell them that you love them? Are you as considerate and thoughtful as you should be? When was the last time you surprised them with a visible show of affection – for example if you are a man when did you last buy your partner something nice like a decent bouquet of flowers? If your partner is not their usual bouncy self do you check if they are feeling under the weather, or are worried about anything?

I have made the point about giving each other your own space, but if you are both retired you will be able to do more things together. Shared treats are really important, as are shared activities.

 **example**

One couple I know decided to take up golf together, and it has become a passion for both of them and has reinvigorated their relationship. I wish I could be as positive about playing bridge together, but I fear this can sometimes be a shortcut to the divorce courts.

Children and grandchildren

Now this might upset you, for which I am sorry, but here is one of my golden rules:

> *Do not expect support from your children; be grateful for what support they offer.*

You do not have children so that they can look after you in your old age. They did not ask to be born so, although they almost certainly want to help, they do not have a duty to do so. They do not have to repay you for the effort you made to bring them up.

Even if you do not accept my arguments then I will make a purely practical point, which is that if you expect things of your children you will almost certainly end up unhappy, and they could end up resenting you or even in extremis hating you. In particular, if expectation goes as far as being demanding then I would expect everyone to end up unhappy.

Many parents will be in the happy position where some, or all, of their children, nieces and nephews will want to help them. I strongly suggest that offers of help are accepted graciously. I came across cases where parents had to be pressured into accepting help. Even though you may want to preserve your independence, try not to be resistant to offers of help.

 **example**

A common problem, which comes up time and again, is when one child provides most of the support to their parents, and then those parents seem to favour one or more of their other children. Unsurprisingly, this does nothing for the relations between their children.

This advice holds true for most Western cultures. However, there are many other cultures where the customs are so different that they make it inappropriate.

Financial help

 **tip**

Lending money to family members often leads to problems, so an outright gift is usually better.

It is important to consider your own financial security as a factor when giving financial help to your loved ones. In my research there were many cases where parents had provided much more financial help than they could really afford to. Sadly, there were also a number of situations where children and grandchildren seemed to be taking advantage of their parents' and grandparents' generosity.

An issue that many retired people mentioned was whether they had to be even-handed. If they gave assistance to one child or grandchild, did they have to make an equivalent offer to their siblings? Some addressed this by keeping their wills up to date, to take account of substantial gifts. Most treated one-off gifts as 'special cases' and took the view that if they had a similar circumstance with another child or grandchild in the future, they would try to offer equivalent help. Regardless of what approach you take, I would try and encourage you to not feel guilty – it's your money and you can give money away as and when you think appropriate.

If you are well off then you will have to resolve the difficult issue of how early you start to pass on your wealth. On the one hand, it seems a shame for those who ultimately will inherit your money to wait until they are probably of an age when they do not really need it. On the other hand, you may feel that access to your savings at too early an age will prevent your children and grandchildren from making their way through life 'on their own'. The most common approach I encountered was for well-off people to help children with their first house purchase. None of the people I talked to who had used this approach later wished they had behaved differently.

Looking after grandchildren

A recent newspaper article I read said that in the UK grandparents typically provided three days' childcare per week. This figure indicates that childcare easily can become the dominant activity for retired grandparents. I found that many grandparents were very happy to take on this role but there are a significant number of potential problems, which are well worth highlighting.

Just as I warn parents not to expect their children to support them as they get older, there is a reciprocal danger that children become dependent on their parents to provide childcare services. If as a grandparent your children depend on you, looking after your grandchildren can turn from a delight into a burden.

What is the solution? Yet again, good communication is the best answer. You need to openly discuss any concerns you have with your children, so that they do not inadvertently start taking advantage of you. You also need to lay down your own guidelines – you must not feel that you cannot say

openly discuss any concerns you have with your children

no. It is not selfish for you to want to pursue your own pleasures and ambitions, and you need to allow enough time for you to have a life of your own.

brilliant tips

It is important to let your children decide how to bring up your grandchildren. Make sure that you find out from your children what their philosophy and rules are, in particular clarify how and when you, rather than your children, should discipline your grandchildren. Do not try and impose your own standards and values and, when looking after your grandchildren, do not undermine your children's approach, rules or authority. It may seem like a bit of harmless spoiling to you, but your children may well not see it that way!

Some grandparents are so wary of butting in that they provide less support than they would like to. In such circumstances you should make it clear to your children that they only have to ask.

A number of grandparents warned me that as they got older they found looking after their grandchildren increasingly tiring. In addition, a number of grandparents found the responsibility of looking after their grandchildren more worrying as they got older. This is something that you and your children need to be aware of, and you all need to be ready for the time that the childcare support you offer will need to decline. Also, be alert to the time when you need to stop providing regular childcare, and move to covering just short-term and urgent requirements.

You may find that you are much less happy looking after babies than older children. Alternatively, you may find it difficult to look after your grandchildren until they start developing their own personalities. You need to discuss such issues openly with your children.

brilliant tip

Do be even-handed with the support you offer to your children. It can cause tensions if you lavish more support on one, or more, of your children.

Parents

One of the more unsettling events in anyone's life is when their parents change from being a source of support to becoming dependent on you. Supporting elderly parents was probably the issue that caused the most grief to the retired people I talked to. If your parents become dependent on your help then I can offer the following guidance.

If you have brothers and/or sisters then try and present a united front to your parents. Some parents will try, either consciously or unconsciously, to drive wedges between their children. Life will be much better if you can stay on close terms with your siblings and agree a common approach to handling the needs of your parents. Sadly, it is not uncommon for tensions to grow about the possible future division of the inheritance from your parents' estate. If this does happen to you the best tactic is to drag the issue out into the open. Once money is discussed openly it seems that people tend to behave better.

An extreme example of the desirability of staying close to your siblings is when a decision needs to be taken about whether parents move closer to one of you, or even in extremis whether your parents move in with one of you.

 **example**

Having a parent come to live with you can put a lot of pressure on the whole family. When I was a lad my parents had my irascible grandfather living with us. It put a great strain on my parents' marriage and also it had a very unpleasant effect on myself, my brother and sister.

brilliant tip

If a brother or sister is shouldering the lion's share of the burden to look after your parents, make sure you give them as much support as you can. For example, make sure that they have cover for their holidays. Also remember to show your appreciation – for example, if they happen to live close to your parents that is no reason for you to expect them to shoulder the whole burden.

The most difficult issue that you may face is when your parents ask, or demand, more than you are comfortable to offer. It is definitely worth hinting that you are not happy, for example by reminding your parents of your other responsibilities to your family, your in-laws, or your work, and this may well work for a while. However, there really is no easy answer to this situation. If you decide you must say no, then try to not get wracked by guilt. As I have already made clear it is my view that you do not have a duty to say yes all the time.

> you do not have a duty to say yes all the time

The rest of society

In the UK, and many other countries, the problems of ageism are far less acute than they used to be. As just one example, many employers now fully appreciate the value of mature workers. There are, however, a number of areas where subtle, but damaging, discrimination still occurs. I encourage you to confront such discrimination where you encounter it. I will highlight some areas that were mentioned frequently to me:

- The use of a demeaning style of communication. People may talk to you loudly and slowly, on the assumption that you have impaired hearing and mental abilities. They may address you as 'my dear', 'love' and the like. In these situations a polite request to talk to you like anyone else is not at all inappropriate.

- Some members of the medical profession may treat you differently from a younger person. As a serious and common example, older people have a higher prevalence of depression, but many doctors assume that depression is an inevitable condition of aging. It is not! Insist on getting proper treatment if you suffer from depression, or any other ailment. If you have the money you may decide to go privately, but if you cannot afford that then take a firm line with your doctor and ask explicitly for a referral to a specialist.

- If you need assistance from social services, you should not accept any intimation that what is being offered is charity – it is your right.

- People may assume that because you are retired you have unlimited time to help them. You need to say no to requests for help that will stop you achieving your goals and ambitions for your retired life.

A final thought

Now you are retired you have time that can be invested in creating, maintaining and strengthening your relationships. This can be one of the greatest delights of retirement.

CHAPTER 7

Maintaining your independence

Many retired people have a fear of having to go into a residential home. Experience seems to indicate that this fear is greater than it should be, with most people making a successful adjustment to residential care. One of the reasons that I describe modern times as the golden age of retirement is that many of this book's readers will be comfortable financially, they will have the benefits of modern medical advances and, as this chapter will show, there is lots of technology, products and services that they can purchase that will support them in living an independent life.

brilliant tips

When selecting a residential home, three key issues to look for are: a homely atmosphere, the amount of contact between the care staff and the residents, and also the amount of autonomy and freedom of choice that residents are allowed – the more the better. An excellent source of advice on all housing and residential care issues is the Elderly Accommodation Counsel, whose website is www.eac.org.uk.

If you move into a residential home then you will benefit from maintaining a positive, independent outlook. Engage with the other residents and if there are group activities then join in. Treat it as your home not a hotel, and do not expect to be waited on hand, foot and finger.

Independence is largely an attitude of mind

The key factor in losing your independence is not the lack of your physical abilities, it is your attitude to overcoming the problems caused by failing senses, mobility and other issues linked to aging. During your working life you will have seen that people with a 'can do' attitude seem to thrive, and the same is just as true in retirement.

Where to live?

Many people said that one of the best, or one of the worst, decisions they had taken was to stay in their current house too long, or to move to the wrong/right house in the same locality, or to move to an inappropriate/excellent new district.

Whilst making a rushed decision soon after retirement obviously can lead to mistakes, the dangers of excessive inertia are probably even greater. Time and again I heard of house moves that had been prompted by some emergency. The added pressures of a house move on top of another major problem can be very stressful. Those people who made the decision to move in good time usually were very pleased that they had done so.

I received excellent feedback from retired people moving closer to other members of their family. This is obviously not a panacea, but I found no single case where such a move had been regretted. An added benefit is that such a move tends to bring support issues into the open, and this can be a great benefit in helping retired people maintain their independence as they get older. If something goes wrong and a family member, or members, are close by, then it is much better for you and your family.

However, there were more regrets from people who had moved to rural areas that they had fallen in love with on holiday. Before taking this step it is well worth investigating the local facilities that will be available to you as you get older. Do you have neighbours close to hand? Is there a good community spirit? Is there good public transport? Can you get taxis easily? Are the local health services good? Can you easily find support services for things like house and garden maintenance, barbers, chiropodists, osteopaths, etc.? How near are decent shops? How good are the road and rail links to people you want to visit? Is the area subject to severe weather? Are there plenty of local sources of entertainment?

If you are staying in the same locality then you may be interested to know that I got a lot of very positive feedback from people who had downsized. Advantages that were frequently mentioned included:

- freeing up capital to invest for more income
- reduced running costs
- lower effort to maintain and keep a clean and tidy house and garden
- easier to stay warm
- less of a worry
- better situated, e.g. closer to family, neighbours, local transport and local amenities
- better suited to less able people – fewer steps, sharp inclines, etc.
- availability of support if sheltered accommodation is chosen.

Apart from the disruption of moving, the only significant downside that was often mentioned was that many much-loved possessions had to be disposed of cheaply – often the younger generation of families will not want your hand-me-downs.

Building a good support network

Your family

Many older people receive a lot of support from their families. We have already looked at family support in the previous chapter and here are some additional tips you may find useful:

accept help gracefully

- Accept help gracefully.
- Be willing to consider changes that will make life easier for you and your family – for example, using a motorised wheelchair, having a chair lift fitted, or even moving house to be nearer to a relative.

- Be positive and do not be grumpy. Try to put up with pain and inconvenience stoically.

- Use your money to make life easier for your family. For example use taxis rather than expecting your family always to take you to places. Arrange for someone to look after you so that your children are relaxed about leaving you to go on holiday.

- Do not become unnecessarily dependent. Make your own decisions whenever possible. Contribute to joint decisions. Do not be afraid to surprise your family, for example by arranging to go off on your own.

- Do not be demanding.

- Do not be disappointed when you would like more help than is offered. Ask for extra support in ways that it is easy for your family to say no.

- Try to give support to your family as well as receiving support. For example, listen to their problems as well as telling them yours. If you no longer have a car can you offer the use of your garage to one of your children? If one of the family is throwing a party is there anything you can do to help?

● Be thoughtful. Do not act as if the world revolves around you and your needs.

Do not apply these tips just to your family: most of them apply to your friends, acquaintances and even those people you pay to help you.

Your social network

Your friends and acquaintances frequently will be an important part of your support network. These can be friends, neighbours and acquaintances you have acquired over the years, or they may be part of some grouping, say a local church, walking group, swimmers, bridge players, and the like. I am often impressed by how kind and helpful people will be when someone needs support.

▶ brilliant   example

My wife and I swim every morning. There is a strong social grouping among the swimmers, many of whom are quite elderly (two are over 90!). Recently, when two of the swimmers were hospitalised with falls, the swimmers organised an informal rota for hospital visits.

Perhaps the most important support that your social network can give is less tangible. Their friendship and sound advice can help you maintain a positive outlook. You can find yourself encouraged to do something positive to address a problem – be it a visit to your doctor, or arranging a visit from a plumber or electrician. You will also find your social network a great source of advice and personal recommendations. It is always better to select a tradesman from a personal recommendation, than from an advertisement in the local paper.

 **tip**

At the risk of repeating myself – remember to be a giver of support and not just a recipient.

Support you pay for

Many retired people maintain their independence whilst remaining in their own homes, by employing one or more 'home help on steroids'. In most areas it is relatively straightforward to find sensible, hard-working individuals who will clean, shop and generally help you maintain your independence. In addition there are agencies who provide carers and nurses on an 'as and when' basis – these will be significantly more expensive than employing someone yourself, but can be a very valuable resource to provide cover when your usual carer is on holiday or ill, or when you need short-term or nursing care.

If you employ someone who helps you maintain your independence you need to be aware of the fact that probably you will become friends with your carer. This means that you will have to balance your two roles as employer and friend. Just because you are friends does not mean you cannot criticise the service you receive. For example, if your carer persistently turns up late, especially without calling to let you know, then

brilliant **tip**

Give your carer annual pay rises. It is unfair to make them ask for a raise. Money alone does not buy loyalty, but this sort of professional consideration will make it clear that you know how to behave professionally as an employer and, consequently, will reinforce your position when you require your employee to behave professionally.

you should make it clear that this is unacceptable. The correct approach in such situations is to be 'polite but firm'.

It is worth raising one issue that potentially can cause serious problems. Under no circumstances whatsoever should you mention the possibility that you will make provision for your carer in your will. If your carer mentions the possibility then this is a gross breach of professional behaviour that would, in most cases, be grounds for dismissal. If you choose to keep them on then make it clear that the issue must never be mentioned again. There is a very great danger that the carer may be manipulative and cannot be trusted. In extreme cases they might even be a physical danger to you. For similar reasons I would advise strongly against lending your carer money, or making excessively generous gifts to them.

brilliant tips

If you feel you need full-time support, then it can be cost effective to have your carer live with you, saving them the costs of accommodation. If you go down this route make sure you make good arrangements for the carer to have plenty of time off – they are not your slave! Remember that many care homes have rooms that offer respite care, which you can use to give your carers a rest. Respite care can also be an excellent way of experiencing residential care.

If you are employing a carer regularly then you ignore employment legislation at your peril. Your social services (see the next section) will be able to provide advice on your responsibilities as an employer. It is not a good idea to collude in your carer being a member of the 'black economy'. Most house insurance policies provide proper insurance cover for such carers.

build up a network of service providers

Apart from carers you will want to build up a network of service providers, such as:

- local doctor
- dentist
- osteopath/chiropractor/physiotherapist
- chiropodist
- plumber
- electrician
- builder
- roofer
- car mechanic
- handyman
- gardener
- tree surgeon
- heating engineer
- taxi firm
- hairdresser.

Many of the services that usually are provided centrally (e.g. hairdressers and chiropodists) can be provided at home if you have difficulty visiting them.

 **brilliant** tip

Many local service suppliers give priority to 'good customers'. Once you have found someone good then try to stick with them. Remember to pay your bills promptly – nothing annoys professional service suppliers more than having to chase customers for payment.

There are also excellent services that cover home emergencies, such as plumbing, electrics, drains, gas and water supply problems. These provide 24/7 cover that gives peace of mind and will save you the stress of finding someone in a hurry, or over the weekend, or at Christmas!

The social services

Most countries will have a state-funded mechanism for helping you to maintain your independence. Usually services will be subsidised only if you cannot afford to pay for them yourself. At the time of writing, in the UK, £22,250 is set as the limit on your savings above which you must fund support yourself. In calculating your savings, any equity you have in your house is excluded until you need residential care, when your house may have to be used to fund your care. Be aware that if you release equity from your home this will then count as savings. If you have a spouse they will not lose their home – but you should check the rules carefully as rules and regulations change constantly.

Even if you have more than £22,250 of savings, a considerable amount of expert advice is available free of charge. The entry point in the UK is a 'needs assessment' where an occupational therapist or skilled social worker will assess what help you need to maintain your independence. This assessment is provided at no charge and future advice is not charged for. However, if your savings are above £22,250 you will have to pay for most services yourself.

I have received mixed reports about the effectiveness of the UK system. Everyone seems to agree that the system is well designed and well intentioned. You will, however, be highly dependent on the skill and personality of the social services staff who implement it – but how could this be otherwise? It is also inevitable that the services that can be offered will be constrained by affordability – there will never be enough money.

The UK system does allow others to top up the support you receive and, if you have to go into residential care, the fees can also be topped up by relations or friends. In addition, you can receive either care service or a direct payment that allows you to make your own arrangements.

brilliant tip

If you go into residential care paid for out of your house's equity then you may want to think upfront about what will happen if you live long enough that the equity falls below £22,250. Some care homes will allow you to stay on even if the state pays the statutory minimum fees. You may have relations who will then pay top-up fees. Your social worker will be able to advise you on the options available.

Is it best to think of such things in advance? I am not sure anyone is wise enough to be able to answer this question. I hope if I find myself in this situation I will want to 'eat, drink and be merry, because tomorrow we ...'

If you are not well off but have savings above the £22,250 limit then you have to consider whether it is worth spending, or giving away, sufficient money to qualify for subsidised services.

I hope this section has not depressed you. Knowing what the facts are helps people conquer their fear. As is so often the case, those who treat life's glass as half full can continue to live very full and happy lives even when they find themselves in constrained financial situations.

Products and services

One of the reasons that I think now is the golden age of retirement is that many businesses now fully appreciate the purchasing power of the 'silver surfer' generation. As a result, the number of products and services that target older people has blossomed. Naturally a strong line in products and services has grown up to help you maintain your independence. Consider just some of those products that are aimed at people whose mobility is becoming impaired:

- houses, bungalows and flats that are designed to support people as they grow older
- lightweight manual wheelchairs
- an enormous range of powered scooters and buggies
- a wide range of aids to help you walk
- showers and baths for less able people
- bathroom aids, such as grab handles, seats that fit in standard baths, and the like
- car adaptations for less able drivers and for carrying wheelchairs
- mobile phones with large buttons and clear displays
- phones for those with hearing impairment
- emergency/fall alarm buttons
- excellent spectacle lenses and magnifiers for those with failing sight
- digital hearing aids
- chair lifts
- gardening tools for the less able
- a wide range of audio books
- electronic book readers that can magnify text
- computers that can cope with visual impairment.

If you add in the increasing range of services available, the support on offer becomes even more impressive and includes:

- holiday accommodation and cruises that cater for the less able

- taxi firms that can transport less able people

- numerous personal services that can be carried out in your own home – hairdressing, chiropody, alternative therapies, etc.

- many services can now be accessed over the telephone or via a computer

- a vast range of products available by post

- 24/7 support for home emergencies, such as plumbing, electrics and drains

- many garages that will collect your car for service and repair.

 **tip**

Do investigate what products are available and, if you can afford them, then do use them to maintain your independence. If you are financially constrained then social services will be able to provide many services free or at a subsidised cost.

One particular area that is worth highlighting is those transport products and services that allow you to get around.

Many people can continue driving safely into their late eighties and nineties. Having access to a car is ideal – even if you are not comfortable driving long distances or in the dark, a car gives you a great deal of independence. If you can drive then make sure you keep in practice; it is short-sighted always to rely on others to drive because they may not always be around to drive you. If you or your partner are disabled then make sure you apply for a disabled person's parking disc because it will make parking very much easier.

it is short-sighted always to rely on others to drive

 **tip**

Drivers need to be on the look out for the time when they are no longer safe enough to carry on driving. If you hurt someone you probably will never forgive yourself.

If you cannot drive, or do not like to drive long distances, then trains or coaches provide cheap and convenient transport for retired people. Senior citizen railcards and bus passes provide substantial savings on travel costs. If you are disabled you should enquire about help making transfers, because there is often a lot of support available.

brilliant **tip**

Do not give up going out or travelling just because it is more of an effort than it used to be. Time and again I was told how train and coach operators, airlines, etc. were charming and helpful when assistance was requested, especially when help was asked for in advance. If things go wrong, almost always you can rely on local staff and members of the public to help you – you often just need to ask.

If you want to travel abroad then the major (non-budget) airlines tend to provide support to customers with impaired mobility.

If you do not have access to a car then this is not the end of the world. For example, the annual cost of running even a small car will pay for a great many taxi journeys. I have previously recommended that you develop a good relationship with a local taxi firm, because they will then go out of their way to be helpful to you – and if they do not then find one who will!

In addition there are many areas with community transport and dial-a-ride services. Sadly, one area where people often had difficulty was in getting support for journeys to and from hospital, and many people said they usually had to make their own arrangements.

Disabled access to transport facilities and other public places has improved dramatically in the late 1990s and into this century, and good progress is still being made. Not everywhere can be made disabled-friendly, but most venues will tell you what facilities are available and very few major facilities have a 'don't care' attitude. You can help yourself by checking out facilities in advance. One issue that was mentioned frequently was that many restaurants and cafés do not, and often cannot, provide ground-floor tables and toilet facilities. However, as one person told me, 'It is better to think about how many restaurants you can visit, rather than how many you cannot.'

New technology

Those retired people who had embraced new technology were effusive about the help it had provided in maintaining their independence. I would not go so far as to say that many retired people actually liked the technology, but they really appreciated what it did for them.

Computers

If you do not already have a home PC you will find the benefits enormous. There will be plenty of local courses to help you get started. You will also find your younger relatives are often very keen to help you, especially when the bloody computer misbehaves. You will also be able to buy computer support over the telephone, and there will most likely be local shops who will repair broken systems.

Why am I so keen on the retired getting a home PC? The support it can offer to your independence can hardly be overstated.

The range of products and services that be accessed over the internet truly is vast. You can do everything from buying groceries to buying the most specialist items, or buying second-hand goods. The supermarket we use even allows you to book a two-hour slot for delivery. The information, both visual and textual, about what you are buying is usually comprehensive, and online feedback often will help you assess what is the best product for you. The internet is such an interconnected world that news of bad service spreads like wildfire and, as a result, the quality of service frequently is excellent – even at bargain-basement prices.

The world wide web is an amazing source of information – on just about everything! It is now often the default mechanism for publishing information. For example, the government increasingly will use the web as the primary channel for disseminating information about what services it offers to you.

 **example**

I can still remember the surprise when an elderly relative's train was delayed and he apologised for keeping me waiting to pick him up at the station, and I said I had checked the arrival and departures board on my computer, so I had known he would be late.

The web increasingly is being used to create communities.

● Communicating by email (electronic letters that usually are delivered in seconds or minutes) is now second nature to most families and friends, with emails also being used to send pictures, videos, documents, jokes, and the like.

- Many of the younger generation will be using social networking sites or blogs (web diaries); these increasingly will be used by them to send people they know news about what they are doing.

- Voice over the internet increasingly is being used to provide cheap or free international telephone calls to friends and relatives.

- Many hobbies have very active online communities. For example, if you want to research your family tree then the internet will be an invaluable tool.

- Increasingly you can take a portable computer and have wireless access to the internet in many public places, hotels and the like.

Get a relative or friend to show you what you can do with a computer; you will be amazed. There are so many things I cannot imagine coping without: street and road maps that can find any postcode or place name and will soon show pictures of the street scenes; routefinders that give detailed directions and time estimates for journeys; rainfall radar maps to show where it is raining or snowing; instant news and analysis from around the world; replay TV and radio programmes you missed; Google Earth, which provides high-definition satellite pictures of anywhere in the world; Wikipedia, the online encyclopedia, covers everything from Proust to Harry Potter; online banking and access to stockbrokers and analyst information; managing your personal finances; online auctions; writing and storing letters; making and printing your own party invitations and greeting cards; digital photography with instant download, viewing and printing of pictures plus the ability to enlarge and crop photos, organise photo albums and the like (and the same for videos); photocopying; scanning old photos and documents … the list is almost endless.

However, there are some dangers that you need to be aware of. Protecting your computer from viruses and criminals is essential. If you do not protect your computer properly you will be attacked – this is not protection against some unlikely event, you probably will be attacked in hours or days. You need to do the following:

● Obtain a virus checker that receives immediate online updating against new viruses.

● Install a piece of software called a firewall, or ensure that if one comes with your computer it is configured properly (you can ask a friend, relative, or computer support person to do this for you).

● Ensure that you enable online security updates to the computer software (the latest versions of Microsoft Windows allow this to be done very easily).

You also need to find out about, and be alert for, the signs of computer scams and virus attacks. Your bank or building society will never ever, ever, ask you to disclose your passwords except when you log on directly to their sites – if they seem to be asking you then it is a criminal committing a crime called phishing. Emails that tell you that you can get free money by helping someone get money out of their country (the so-called Nigerian scam), or who tell you that you have won a competition, are all from con artists. If something seems too good to be true, it is indeed too good to be true. Emails you do not fully recognise, such as an email telling you a package cannot be delivered, or that invite you to click on a web link that will tell you more, usually are from con artists or activate viruses. Any email in broken English should be very suspect. Stilted offers from abroad to buy goods that you are selling are from con artists – personally I refuse to sell any items abroad even if the buyer appears to be genuine.

 **tip**

If in any doubt whatsoever do not reply and do not click on a web link. Once you have used a computer for a while you will recognise immediately dangerous approaches.

The second major risk you need to be aware of is the need to protect your data in the event that your computer hard disk (which stores your data) breaks down and the data from the disk cannot be recovered. There are numerous ways of dealing with this risk easily and cheaply.

- Most modern computers have an automated facility that regularly will make a copy of your files onto a separate disk that is plugged into your computer. Such disks are not expensive, and you need to make sure you specify this when you buy a new computer.

- You can copy important data regularly onto CDs or DVDs – well worth doing if you have an elderly computer. Alternatively you can email valuable data to a website that offers data storage facilities.

- Increasingly you can avoid storing any data on your computer but instead use software that is run on websites, which also will store your data securely on their computers. Remarkably, most of this software will be free – it is paid for by advertisers placing adverts on the websites. Documents, pictures and virtually all sorts of data can be managed in this way. This approach is referred to by the phrase 'cloud computing' and, in my opinion, this is going to become an increasingly popular and easy-to-use way of accessing applications and storing data via the internet.

 **tip**

Trust me, if you do not protect your data it is only a matter of time before you lose it all.

Games consoles

The latest generation of games machines, pioneered by the Nintendo Wii, allows physical interaction with games in a safe virtual environment. Games such as tennis, golf, baseball, skiing, yoga, aerobics, etc. provide a fun way to improve your flexibility, balance, reactions, timing, dexterity and fitness. These machines also allow group activity, which friends and the whole family can enjoy.

Mobile phones

Mobile phones mean that now you can contact your friends and relatives (almost) anywhere and anytime. They provide an excellent way to call for assistance if something goes wrong while you are away from your home. They provide a good back up in case your home phone line breaks down. They provide a cheap way to stay in contact when in hotels or when in residential care. If you find modern phones too small and fiddly, then there are phones available with large buttons and clear displays.

Satellite navigation

A number of elderly drivers told me that sat nav had enabled them to keep driving long distances for a longer period of time than would have been possible without it. The technology also alerts you to the locations of speed cameras, which is a great help now that the UK roads have such a vast number of different speed limits that it can be confusing as to what the speed limit is at any given location. In addition, many sat navs can be used to guide you when you are a pedestrian, or to provide position location when walking in the country.

Telemedicine

At the time this book is being written (2009) there is a lot of interest in the possibilities of telemedicine. Telemedicine uses sensors and modern communications to alert someone who can help you if your physical condition deteriorates significantly. For example, it should be possible for someone with a heart condition to wear a sensor that will alert the emergency services if they have a heart attack. Only time will tell if this becomes a significant technology for helping people maintain their independence. Fall alarms are a simple, but very valuable, first step in telemedicine.

Health services

We have already looked at many of the issues around health in Chapter 5, but here are some more tips that you can use to get the best out of the medical services available to you.

● Most people leave it too long before going to see their doctor about a medical problem. Doctors are often depressed that they see a patient only when things have become serious, and earlier treatment would have been much easier and avoided lasting damage. For chronic problems, you should talk to your doctor about whether a second opinion from a consultant is worthwhile.

● Most people do not prepare properly when going to see their doctor. What precisely are your symptoms? How severe are they? When do they occur? Where and how do they manifest themselves? If you have pain, how would you describe it? Is there any relevant history the doctor needs to know about?

Have you had a similar problem before? Have you had previous conditions that could be relevant?

brilliant tip

I would not recommend that you attempt self-diagnosis using the internet. Your doctor will be very much better at diagnosis than you are. In addition, you will start imagining that you have other symptoms. However, if you find that you do have significant other symptoms then mention them to the doctor.

- Hearing and remembering what the doctor or consultant says to you is very difficult. Thinking of the right questions to ask on the spur of the moment is also very hard, so it is best to take a written list of questions with you. If possible, take somebody in with you because they will observe and hear things you may miss and can prompt you to ask relevant questions. If you have to go alone, then take a pencil and paper to make notes.

  take a written list of questions with you

- If treatment is recommended then for goodness sake follow the advice given to you. If it says take pills with food then there is a good reason for that. If it says take three times a day, then take the medicine three times a day. Read the instructions that come with the medicine, and follow them. Read the side effects, but do not get paranoid. I do not apologise for lecturing you because research shows that a very significant number of patients do not do as they are told!

- If you do have a significant health problem the internet can be an excellent source of information about how best to overcome it or live with it. Most doctors do not mind discussing treatment options with patients who have researched their health problem. Check that you are obtaining information from reputable websites (check the 'about us' section of the sites) and cross check between sites. Treat personal comments on the internet from individuals with a large pinch of salt.

● Most doctors' surgeries have in-house nurses and district nurses. The feedback I have received about such nurses and district nurses was consistently excellent. If you have a health problem then the district nurses can be key to keeping you in your own home.

● Pharmacists often are very knowledgeable. They also tend to have more time to talk to you than your local doctor. Their wide experience often will be a mine of useful advice. For example, if you do not tolerate a particular drug very well they may well be able to recommend that you ask your doctor to try a different medication. Pharmacists usually offer services to obtain, make up and deliver repeat prescriptions.

● If you have a serious health problem, such as cancer, blindness or severe disability, then there are many charities who will be happy to help you.

brilliant tip

It can be useful to write down what medication you take and when you take it. This will enable carers to ensure that you take the right medication. It can also be worth writing down key aspects that carers need to know about – such as food intolerances and the like.

Final words

I n these last few pages I wanted to draw out what I think are a few of the key issues that can help you enjoy a long and happy retirement.

Maintain a positive outlook

Almost everyone has their cross to bear. Indeed many people I talked to had to cope with many different, serious problems. These might well relate to health, or lack of money, or the burden of looking after elderly parents – or any number of other problem areas.

If I had to identify the single most important lesson I learnt from writing this book it was that those people who maintained a positive outlook could overcome almost any problem. These people ruled their problems, they never let their problems rule their lives.

> those people who maintained a positive outlook could overcome almost any problem

When I first started my research I was somewhat fatalistic: I believed that you were born either an optimist or a pessimist and hence you were the victim of your genes. However, it became clear to me that you can consciously develop a more positive outlook. If you force yourself to say positive things, and do positive things, you will almost certainly start feeling more positive.

 **tip**

> Do not let the little problems in life get you down. The washing machine or car breaking down is not the end of the world. Count your blessings: you do not have to solve these little problems while holding down a stressful job.

One aspect that came up time and again in my conversations with retired people was the fear of having to go into residential care. Although most people make a successful transition into residential care, most people want to maximise the time they can stay in their own home. Maintaining your independence is as much (or more) a matter of keeping a positive outlook as it is about the state of your physical abilities. The next point further highlights how important psychological issues are.

Develop a new persona

One of the biggest shocks the newly retired find is that their previous persona usually was tied closely to their working life – for example 'I am a partner in a solicitors'. After retirement many people found a terrible sense of loss of their previous identity. You need to develop a new identity, even if it is 'I don't know how I ever found time to work'. The only people I talked to who got bored were those who could not find a new persona, and they usually solved this problem by getting themselves a new job – either paid or in the voluntary sector.

> you need to develop a new identity

Strongly allied to your identity and feelings of self-worth will be your dreams and ambitions. You should not feel that you have to have big dreams and ambitions, but retirement is a time when a lot of people find they have the space to push their lives in new directions. It is important to realise that most retired people have no trouble at all filling their time. Consequently, you may well need to prioritise your activities to give you time to pursue your dreams.

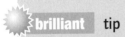 **tip**

Part of your work persona was the way you dressed for work. Now this has gone you may benefit from developing a new style of dressing for your retirement. As a personal example, I have never worn clothes with such fashionable labels as I now pick up from charity shops – what my wife calls 'charity shop chic'.

Grow your social network

Your friends and acquaintances will prevent you from becoming lonely, will help you maintain a positive outlook, will be a source of advice and support, will stop you becoming self-centred, and will provide opportunities to get out and enjoy yourself. You need to make the time to stay in touch, offer hospitality and provide advice and support to others. If you are naturally introverted then you need to make a positive effort to make new contacts and maintain existing ones.

make a positive effort to make new contacts and maintain existing ones

 **tip**

Try to be a good listener.

Develop a healthy lifestyle

There is a lot of truth in the saying that 'you are what you eat'. You now have the time to eat a healthy diet, and to eat the number of calories that given the exercise you take will keep you at a weight that you are happy with. You also have the time to take enough exercise to keep fit and trim. If you do not fancy swimming or working out in a gym then walk – most people can. Everyone I talked to who had tackled their eating habits and their exercise regime felt more energised, had a better self-image, and research shows they are likely to have much longer, more active lives. You know it makes sense!

Understand money issues

Now you have lost your main salary you probably will have to be more careful with money. Time and again, retired people told me how cheaply they now lived. You can reduce your discretionary expenditure, shop more cheaply, organise your car ownership more cost effectively and you do not have many work-related expenses. It is well worth doing at least one budget to see where the money goes – I can guarantee that you will find large savings that can be made easily.

It is little short of a scandal that financial advisers who provide 'free' advice make their money from commissions on the products they advise you to buy. This system virtually guarantees that you will not get the best advice.

To counter this I have given a lot of advice and information on how to invest your savings. You need to understand money matters, because once savings are gone they are often impossible to replenish. I have explained how safe investments inevitably will lead to inflation eroding your savings. There is little alternative to investing a substantial part of your savings in

> you need to understand money matters

the stock market or corporate bonds. Regular saving into the stock market is best, but you need to understand timing issues when you have lump sums to invest or you want to buy corporate bonds. To help you I have explained timing issues in some detail. It is a sad fact of life that often you are best investing when the economic outlook in the stock market seems blackest.

brilliant tip

When the stock market drops and your portfolio loses a significant part of its value – do not panic! The stock market is cyclic and it will come back up again eventually (provided you have not done something silly like investing in an investment bubble).

Give your partner space

If you have a partner then your retirement is going to disrupt their life significantly. Just because they enjoyed your company during holidays does not mean that you will not now destroy their established routines. Make sure you do not crowd them and be considerate as you both develop new routines.

You can say no to your family

No matter how much you want to help look after elderly parents and grandchildren, you do not have to be at their beck and call always – you are entitled to your own life as well.

brilliant tip

The key to solving many difficult relationship issues is simple – you need to discuss problems openly.

Listen to other family members' views but also be firm but kind about what you can offer.

As a parent do not expect or demand support from your children. Be pleased and grateful for what is offered. When asking for extra help make it easy for your children to say no. You do not have children so that they can look after you in your old age.

Stay in touch with reality

It is very easy for retired people to become remote from the realities and pressures of the real world. Try to mix with young people and listen to what they have to say. Stay abreast of current events, sample the latest cultural trends and embrace new technology. Try not to become a grumpy old man/woman.

try to mix with young people

A final word

If there is a golden rule of retirement it is 'use it or lose it'. The more you do, mentally and physically, the more you will want to do, and the more you will be able to do. Retirement should be the best time of your life, so make sure you make the most of it. This book should help you identify all the good things that are possible, and avoid or solve the problems you will encounter.

use it or lose it